HTML

Cheat Sheet

(Cover all Basic Html Syntaxes,

More Than 300 Examples)

Ray Yao

About This Book

This book covers all basic HTML syntaxes, almost each syntax entry lists a program example and result output. (**350 entries, 350 examples, 350 outputs**). We can quickly reference the most helpful programming syntaxes, such as common command syntax, html tag syntax, html attribute syntax, html event syntax and Css syntax……; all these syntaxes are very useful for programming.

We can take this book as a basic syntax manual because its entries are arranged alphabetically so that we can easily reference the important syntax. This book also includes the basic CSS syntax related to HTML.

"350 entries, 350 examples, 350 outputs" is the unique feature of this book.

Disclaimer

This book is intended as a basic syntax manual only; it cannot include all entries on this subject. Its purpose is as a supplement for a cheat sheet book, not as a whole HTML dictionary.

Table of Contents

Syntax Chart

@import syntax:

@import "myStyle.css";
// import the external css style files to the current html file.
e.g.
// Assume that there are three following external css files in the same folder with myFile.html.
1. myStyle1.css
h1{color:purple; font-family: Times new roman}
2. myStyle2.css
h2{color:orange; font-family:arial}
3. myStyle3.css
h3{color:blue; font-family:arial narrow}
4. myFile.html // this is a html document
<html>
<style >
@import "myStyle1.css";
@import "myStyle2.css";
@import "myStyle3.css";
</style>
<h1>This is heading1</h1>
<h2>This is heading2</h2>
<h3>This is heading3</h3>
</html>
// Output:

This is heading1

This is heading2
This is heading3

<!-- --> syntax:

<!-- html comment -->
// The <!-- --> is a comment symbol of html
// PHP or HTML compiler always ignores the html comment.
e.g.
<html>
Hello World! **<!-- show Hello World! -->**
</html>
// Output: Hello World!

<!DOCTYPE> syntax:

<!DOCTYPE html>
</html>
// Define the html document type.
// All html documents should start with a <!DOCTYPE> declaration.
e.g.
<!DOCTYPE html>
<html>

<body>
The document contents are in here......
</body>
</html>
// Output: The document contents are in here......

<a href> syntax:

<a href="url">Go to example.com</a>
// Create a hyperlink
e.g.
<a href="https://www.amazon.com"**>**Go to Amazon.com**</a>**
// Output: Go to Amazon.com

<a> javascript syntax:

<a href = "javascript : function()">
// Using a specifier "javascript:" can call a JavaScript function.
e.g.
<a href = "**javascript:alert('Hello! Hyperlinks.')**">Click Here</a>
// Output: Hello! Hyperlinks.

<a> mailto syntax:

<a href = "mailto:xxx@xxx.com"> text </a>
// Activate the default email client application on the computer for sending an e-mail.
e.g.
<a href = "**mailto: rayyao@myemail.com**">Email to RayYao</a>
// Output: **Email to RayYao**

<a target> syntax:

< a target = "_blank / _self / _parent / _top">
// "_blank": another new page will be opened in a new tab.
// "_self": a self page will be opened on its original window.
// "_parent": a target page will be opened in a parent frame.
// "_top": a target page will be opened in the topmost frame.
e.g.
<a href="http://www.amazon.com" **target="_self"**>To Amazon</a>
<a href="http://www.google.com" **target="_blank"**>To Google</a>
// Output: To Amazon To Google

<abbr> syntax:

<abbr title="Original Text">abbreviation/acronym</abbr>
// Define an abbreviation or an acronym, such as "AJAX", "ASAP"…
e.g.
This is the **<abbr title=**"World Trade Organization"**>**WTO**</abbr>**
// Output: This is the WTO

<address> syntax:

<address>
contact information
</address>

// Define the contact information of the owner of a document
e.g.
```
<address>
Visit us at:<br>
168 Washington Ave.<br>
Los Angeles, California<br>
USA
</address>
```
// Output:
Visit us at:
168 Washington Ave.
Los Angeles, California
USA

<area> syntax:

```
<img src=" " width="" height="" usemap="#mapName"/>
<map name="mapName">
<area shape=""  coords=""  href=""  alt="">
</map>
```
// <area> defines a clickable area inside the <map> element, the <area> can redirect a page to another specified page.
// <map> defines an image map which contains the <area> elements.
// "usemap" specifies that the image is applied to <map> by map name.
// "shape" specifies the shape of the area.
// "coords" specifies the coordinates of an area in an image map.
// "href" sets the url of the page. "alt" sets an alternate text.
e.g.
```
<img src="pic.jpg" width="300" height="120" usemap="#myMap"/>
  <map name="myMap">
    <area shape="poly"  coords="59,31,28,83,91,83"
          href="c#.htm"  alt="poly">
    <area shape="circle"  coords="155,56,26"
          href="ruby.htm"  alt="circle">
    <area shape="rect"  coords="224,30,276,82"
          href="java.htm"  alt="rectangle">
  </map>
```
// Output:

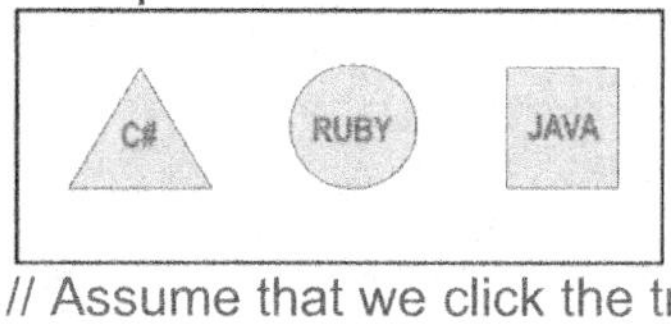

// Assume that we click the triangle(c#) area, it will redirect the page to the c#.html page.

<article> syntax:

```
<article>
 text
</article>
```
// Define an independent text content
e.g.

<article>
<h2>Java</h2>
<p>"Java in 8 Hours" is a book for programming beginners</p>
</article>
<article>
<h2>Ruby</h2>
<p>"Ruby in 8 Hours" is a book for high school & college students</p>
</article>
// Output:
Java
"Java in 8 Hours" is a book for programming beginners
Ruby
"Ruby in 8 Hours" is a book for high school & college students

---

<aside> syntax:

<aside> text </aside>
// Define some additional information about the main contents, such as explanation, biography, profile, history…
e.g.
<h3>Cantonese Language</h3>
<aside>
<p>Cantonese is a language with a history of thousands of years, it is spoken in Canton, Hong Kong, Macau, and Southern area of China.</p>
</aside>
// Output:
Cantonese Language
Cantonese is a language with a history of thousands of years, it is spoken in Canton, Hong Kong, Macau, and Southern area of China.

<audio controls> syntax:

<audio width="" height="" controls>
<source src="audio_file" type="audio/mpeg">
</audio>
// Embed an audio control to the current page
e.g.
<audio width="300" height="50"controls>
<source src="myMusic.mp3" type="audio/mpeg">
</audio>
// Output:

<b> syntax:

<b>This is a bold text. </b>
// Show text in a bold font
e.g.
Note: **<b>**This is a bold text. **</b>**
// Output: *Note:* **This is a bold text.**

<base> syntax:

<base href="url" target="">
// Set a default url and a default target for all <a> links on a page.
// "target" means _blank, _parent, _self, _top.
e.g.
<head>
<base href="https://www.amazon.com/" target="_blank">
</head>
<body>
<**a** href=" ">To Amazon</a>
</body>
// Output: To Amazon

<bdi> syntax:

<bdi>special_text</bdi>
// "bdi" means bidirectional Isolation.
// <bdi> isolates the text which may have special format.
e.g.
<p>
This content **<bdi>?????</bdi>** may be written in Chinese language
</p>
// Output:
This content ????? may be written in Chinese language

<bdo> syntax:

<bdo dir="ltr"> text </bdo> // character order from left to right
<bdo dir="rtl"> text </bdo> // character order from right to left
// Set the direction of the character sequence.
e.g.
<bdo dir="rtl">The direction of this text is from right to left.**</bdo>**
// Output: .tfel ot thgir morf si txet siht fo noitcerid ehT

<big> syntax:

<big>This is a big text. </big>
// Show text in a big font
e.g.
Note: **<big>**This is a big text. **</big>**
// Output: *Note:* **This is a big text.**

<blockquote> syntax:

<blockquote cite="url">
// Define a block of code that is quoted from another web site.
e.g.
<p>Here is a quote from Ray Yao's website:</p>
<blockquote cite="www.amazon.com/author/ray-yao">
We sell both Paperbacks and Kindle books,
the searching keywords are:
Xxxxxx by Ray Yao
</blockquote>
// Output:

Here is a quote from Ray Yao's website:
We sell both Paperbacks and Kindle books, the searching keywords are:
Xxxxxx by Ray Yao

<body> syntax:

<body> contents </body>
// Define the body of an html document.
e.g.

```
<html>
<body>
Hello World!
</body>
</html>
```

// Output: Hello World!

---

 syntax:

**
**
// The <br> tag defines a line break.
e.g.

```
<body>
This is the first line.
<br>
This is the second line.
<br>
This is the third line.
</body>
```

// Output:
This is the first line.
This is the second line.
This is the third line.

<button> syntax:

<button type="button" onclick="alert('Clicked!')">Click Me</button>
// Used with the <button> element to create a clickable button that can perform various actions, such as triggering JavaScript functions or submitting forms.
e.g.

```
<form>
  <button type="button" onclick="alert('Button clicked!')">Click Me</button>
</form>
```

// Output:	Click Me

<canvas> syntax:

<canvas id = "myCanvas" width = "" height = ""></canvas>
// It can be used to draw graphs, do photo jobs or make simple animations by using JavaScript.
e.g.

```
<style>
#myCanvas{border:10px solid green;}
</style>
<canvas id = "myCanvas" width = "80" height = "40"></canvas>
```

// Output:

<caption> syntax:

<caption>Table Caption</caption>
// Display the caption of the table
e.g.
<caption>Table Caption</caption>
<tr>
<td>Cell 1</td>
<td>Cell 2</td>
<td>Cell 3</td>
</tr>
// Output:

Table Caption

Cell 1	Cell 2	Cell 3

<circle> syntax:

<circle cx="" cy="" r="" stroke="" stroke-width="" fill="color"/>
// Create a circle in svg.
// "cx", "cy": the x and y coordinates of the circle center. "r": circle radius.
// "stroke": circle border. "stroke-width": circle border width
e.g.
<svg width="120" height="120">
<**circle** cx="60" cy="60" r="50" stroke="red" stroke-width="3" fill="yellow"/>
</svg>

// Output: 

<cite> syntax:

<cite>Title</cite>
// Cite a title of book, song, music, painting, website......
e.g.
<p>
<cite> PHP Cheat Sheet **</cite>** by Ray Yao, Published in 2022.
</p>
// Output
PHP Cheat Sheet by Ray Yao, Published in 2022.

<code> syntax:

<code> source_code <code>
// Display a piece of source code.
e.g.
<code>
var myVariable = "Hello World";

```
alert (myVariable);  <br>
</code>
// Output:
var myVariable = "Hello World";
alert (myVariable);
```

<col> syntax:

```
<col style="property:value">
// Set the style of a column
// <col> is used inside the <colgroup> </colgroup>.
e.g.
<table>
  <colgroup>
    <col style="background-color:orange">
    <col style="background-color:yellow">
  </colgroup>
  <tr>
   <th>C#</th> <th>C++</th>
  </tr>
  <tr>
   <td>Cheat Sheet</td> <td>In 8 Hours</td>
  </tr>
</table>
// Output:
```

C#	C++
Cheat Sheet	In 8 Hours

<colgroup> syntax:

```
<colgroup>
     <col style="property:value">
     <col style="property:value">
</colgroup>
// Set the style of a group of columns
// <col> is used inside the <colgroup> </colgroup>
e.g.
<table>
  <colgroup>
    <col style="background-color:orange">
    <col style="background-color:yellow">
  </colgroup>
  <tr>
   <th>C#</th> <th>C++</th>
  </tr>
  <tr>
   <td>Cheat Sheet</td> <td>In 8 Hours</td>
  </tr>
</table>
// Output:
```

<data> syntax:

```
<data value=""> text </data>
```

// Allow you to add your own data to tags.

e.g.

```
<ol>
  <li><data value="green">Apple</data></li>
  <li><data value="yellow">Banana</data></li>
  <li><data value="red">Cherry</data></li>
</ol>
```

// Output:

1. Apple
2. Banana
3. Cherry

<datalist> syntax:

```
<datalist id="">
  <option value="">
  <option value="">
</datalist>
```

// Define an optional value for an input control.

e.g.

```
<label for="myList">Choose your language in the list:</label><br>
<input list="language" name="myList" id="myList">    // input control
<datalist id="language">
  <option value="JAVA">
  <option value="HTML">
  <option value="RUBY">
</datalist>
```

// Output:

Choose your language in the list:

HTML	v

<del> syntax:

```
<del>This is a del text. </del>
```

// Show text with deleting line

e.g.

```
Note: <del>This is a del text. </del>
```

// Output: *Note:* ~~This is a del text~~

<details> syntax:

```
<details> text </details>
```

// Define a button, show the details texts to describe the topic.

e.g.

```
<p>Click the details button to know about Cantonese language:</p>
<details>
```

<p>Cantonese is a language with a history of thousands of years, it is spoken in Canton, Hong Kong, Macau, and Southern area of China.</p>
</details>
// Output:
Click the details button to know about Cantonese language:
▼ Details
Cantonese is a language with a history of thousands of years, it is spoken in Canton, Hong Kong, Macau, and Southern area of China.

<dfn> syntax:

<dfn> text </dfn>
// Define a term which will be described by the subsequent text in details.
e.g.
<dfn> Cantonese </dfn> is a language with a history of thousands of years, it is spoken in Canton, Hong Kong, Macau, and Southern area of China.
// Output:
Cantonese is a language with a history of thousands of years, it is spoken in Canton, Hong Kong, Macau, and Southern area of China.

<div> syntax:

<div class = "value"> text </div>
<div id = "value"> text </div>
// Group their content elements as blocks for styling purposes.
// <div> can be used as block tag. <span> can be used as inline tag.
e.g.
<style type = "text/css">
.d{font-family: arial; color: blue;}
</style>
<div class = "d">
<i>AAAAA</i> <b>BBBBB</b> <i>CCCCC</o>
</div>
// Output: *AAAAA* **BBBBB** *CCCCC*

<dl>, <dt>, <dd> syntax:

<dl>
<dt>……</dt> <dd>……</dd>
</dl>
// <dl></dl> defines a list, which contains <dt></dt> and <dd></dd>
// <dt></dt> contains the first layer of list items.
// <dd></dd> contains the second layer of list items.
e.g.
<dl>
<dt>The first A layer</dt> <dd>The second A layer</dd>
<dt>The first B layer</dt> <dd>The second B layer</dd>
<dt>The first C layer</dt> <dd>The second C layer</dd>
</dl>
// Output:
The first A layer
The second A layer

The first B layer
                    The second B layer
The first C layer
The second C layer

<ellipse> syntax:

<ellipse cx="" cy="" rx="" ry="" stroke="" stroke-width="" fill=""/>

// Create an ellipse in svg.
// "stroke":ellipse border. "stroke-width":ellipse border width "fill":color

cx	the x coordinate of the center of the ellipse
cy	the y coordinate of the center of the ellipse
rx	the horizontal radius
ry	the vertical radius

e.g.
<svg height="150" width="480">
<ellipse cx="180" cy="70" rx="90" ry="40"
stroke="red" stroke-width="3" fill="yellow"/>
</svg>

// Output: 

<em> syntax:

<em>This is an italic text. </em>

// Show text in an italic font
e.g.
Note: **<em>**This is an italic text. **</em>**
// Output: Note: *This is an italic text*

<embed> syntax:

<embed src = "" width="" height="" loop="" />

// Embed a music or a song to the current page.
// src = "" specifies the url of music file, flash file or movie file.
// "width" and "height" specifies the size of the contents.
// "loop=true/false" set to play music repeatedly.
e.g.
<embed src = "myMusic.mp3" width=300 height=50 loop=true/>
// Output:

<fieldset> syntax:

<fieldset> related_elements </fieldset>

// Group associated elements into a frame.
e.g.
<form action="">
  <fieldset>
    name <input type="text" id="name" name="name">

    age <input type="text" id="age" name="age">

    email <input type="email" id="email" name="email">


```
 </fieldset>
</form>
// Output:
```

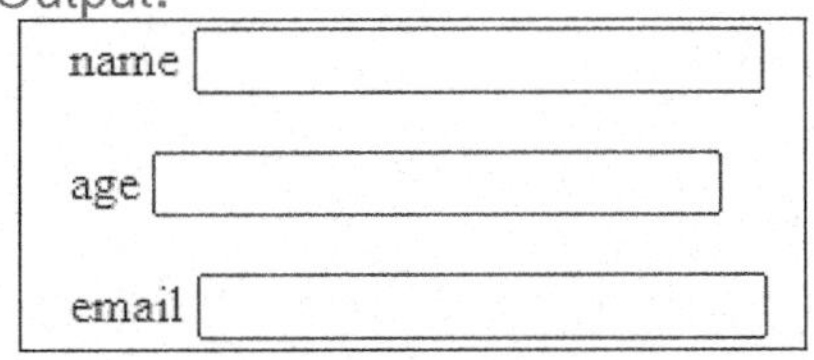

<figcaption> syntax:

```
<figcaption> text </figcaption>
// Define a caption for the <figure> element.
e.g.
<figure>
 <img src="flower.jpg" alt="flower" style="width:50">
 <figcaption>Figure: The logo of Ray Yao's Books</figcaption>
</figure>
// Output:
```

Figure: The logo of Ray Yao's Books

<figure> syntax:

```
<figure> contents </figure>
// Add contents like images, photos, illustrations, diagrams……
e.g.
<figure>
 <img src="flower.jpg" alt="flower" style="width:50">
 <figcaption>Figure: The logo of Ray Yao's Books</figcaption>
</figure>
// Output:
```

Figure: The logo of Ray Yao's Books

<footer> syntax:

```
<footer> text </footer>
// Define a footer of a document or a webpage, which usually contains the
information of author, copyright, email, address, phone number……
e.g.
<body>
<h3>The example of footer:</h3>
<footer>
<i> C++ Cheat Sheet </i>  Author: Ray Yao. All Copyright Reserved.
</footer>
</body>
// Output:
```

The example of a footer:
C++ Cheat Sheet Author: Ray Yao. All Copyright Reserved.

<form> syntax:

<form name="" id="" method="" action="">
……
</form>

// A "form" in html is a very important element, which is used to accept the requests or inputs from the user.
// <form></form> is the form tags.
// name ="" specifies the name of the form.
// id = "" specifies the id of the form.
// method="" specifies the data send by "get" or "post".
// "get" method sends data to the server openly, small quantity.
// "post" method sends data to the server secretly, more quantity.
// action="" specifies the data will be processed by a form handler.
// To learn more how to process data, Please see *PHP Cheat Sheet.*
e.g.
<form name="myForm" method="get" action="myFile.php">
<input type="text" name="myInput" value="Please enter data.">
</form>
// Output:

Please enter data

<h1> - <h6> syntax:

<h> heading </h>

// Create heading element from <h1></h1> to </h6></h6>.
e.g.
<h1>H1 Size</h1>
<h2>H2 Size</h2>
<h3>H3 Size</h3>
<h4>H4 Size</h4>
<h5>H5 Size</h5>
<h6>H6 Size</h6>
// Output:

H1 Size

H2 Size

H3 Size

H4 Size

H5 Size

H6 Size

<head> syntax:

<head> metadata </head>

// Contain the metadata such as document title, character set, meta, styles, links, scripts, information about the web page.

e.g.
<html>
<head>
<meta charset="utf-8"> // metadata
<title>Example of Head</title> // metadata
</head>
<body>
<p>Hello World</p>
</body>
</html>
// Output: Hello World

<header> syntax:

<header> contents </header>
// Define the header of a page or a document. It usually contains a logo, branding, navigational links, etc.
e.g.
<body>
<header>
<nav> Home   About Us   Contact </nav>
</header>
</body>
// Output:
Home About Us Contact

<hr> syntax:

<hr>
// Add a horizontal line in an HTML page.
e.g.
<p>There is a horizontal line under this sentence.</p>
<hr>
<p>This is a horizontal line above this sentence.</p>
// Output:
There is a horizontal line under this sentence.

This is a horizontal line above this sentence.

<html> syntax:

<html> Contents </html>
// Define the beginning and end of an html document.
e.g.
<html>
<body>
<p>Hello World</p>
</body>
</html>
// Output: Hello World

<i> syntax:

<i>This is an italic text. </i>

// Show text in an italic font
e.g.
Note: **<i>**This is an italic text. **</i>**
// Output: Note: *This is an italic text*

<iframe> syntax:

<iframe src="source" width="" height=""> </iframe>
// Embed a frame with the specified width and height.
// src="source" specifies an embedded file or website.
e.g.
<iframe src = "http://www.usa.com" width="500" height="350" scrolling=yes>
</iframe>
// Output:

<img> syntax:

<img src = "" width = "" height = "" alt = "">
// Insert an image by image name, width, height
// "src" sets image name, "alt" sets an alternate text.
e.g.
<**img** src = "flower.jpg" width = "100" height = "80"
alt = "This is a flower.">
// Output:

<input type = "button"> syntax:

<input type = "button" name= "" id="" value="" onclick="">

// Button can be used to input data by user.

// type = "button" specifies the input type as "button".

// value="" displays the text on the button.

// "onclick=function()" runs the function when the button is clicked.
e.g.
<form>
<input **type = "button"** name= "myButton" value="Click Me"
onclick = 'alert("OK!")'> // run alert() when the button is clicked
</form>
// Output:

Click Me

<input type="checkbox"> syntax:

<input type="checkbox" id="" name="" value="">

// Check box can be used to select multiple options by user
// type = "checkbox" specifies the input type as "checkbox".
// One or more check boxes can be selected at the same time.

e.g.

<form action="myFile.php"> // php file processes the inputted data
Coffee <input **type="checkbox"** name="chb" value="coffee">
Milk <input **type="checkbox"** name="chb" value="milk">
Sugar <input **type="checkbox"** name="chb" value="sugar">
<input type = "submit" name= "sbmt" value="Submit" >
</form>
// Output:

Coffee ☑ Milk ☑ Sugar ☐ Submit

<input type="color"> syntax:

<input type="color" name="" id="" value="#xxxxxx">

// Define a color picker, allow user to choose one color.

e.g.

<form action="myFile.php"> // php file processes the inputted data
Please click the color picker to choose one color:
<input **type="color"** name="c" id="c" value="#000000">
</form>
// Output:

Please click the color picker to choose one color:

<input type="date"> syntax:

<input type="date" name="" id="">

// Define a date picker, allow user to choose one date.

e.g.

<form action="myFile.php"> // php file processes the inputted data
Please click the date picker to choose one date:
<input **type="date"** name="d" id="d">
</form>
// Output: Please click the date picker to choose one date:

mm/dd/yyyy

<input type="datetime"> syntax:

<input type="datetime" name="" id="">

// Define a datetime picker, allow user to choose one datetime.

e.g.

<form action="myFile.php"> // php file processes the inputted data
Please click the datetime picker to choose one datetime:
<input **type="datetime-local"** name="d" id="d">
</form>

// Output: Please click the datetime picker to choose one datetime:

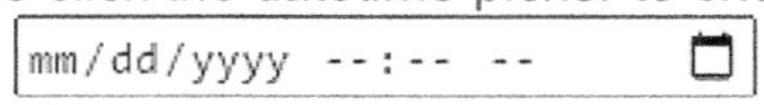

<input type="email"> syntax:

<input type="email" name="" id="">

// Define an email field which can validate the email when submitted

e.g.

```
<form action="myFile.php">  // php file processes the inputted data
Please enter your email:<br>
<input type="email" name="e" id="e" >  <input type="submit">
</form>
```

// Output: Please enter your email:

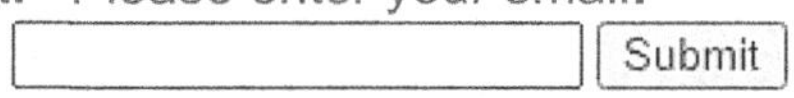

<input type="file"> syntax:

<input type="file" name="" id="">

// type = "file" specifies the input type as "file" which is used to upload files to the server.

e.g.

```
<form action="myFile.php" method="post" enctype="multipart/form-data">
// php file processes the inputted data
Please upload a file:<br><br>
<input type="file" name="upload"><br><br>
<input type = "submit" name= "sbmt" value="Upload" >
</form>
```

// Output:

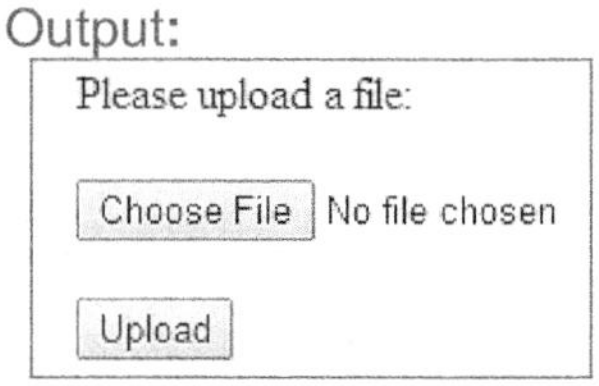

<input type="hidden"> syntax:

<input type="hidden" id="" name="" value="">

// The "Hidden Inputs" is an invisible control, but it is used to send data.

// type = "hidden" specifies the input type as "hidden".

e.g.

```
<form action="myFile.php">  // php file processes the inputted data
Coffee <input type="checkbox" name="chb" value="coffee">
Milk <input type="checkbox" name="chb" value="milk">
Sugar <input type="checkbox" name="chb" value="sugar">
<input type="hidden" name="hdn" value="cream">
<input type = "submit" name= "sbmt" value="Submit" >
</form>
```

// Output:

// Explanation: You can only see the Coffee, Milk and Sugar checkbox, but you cannot see the Cream checkbox, because it is hidden.

When the “Submit” button is clicked, all selected data on the form, including “cream” value will be submitted. myFile.php will process the submitted data.

<input type="month"> syntax:

<input type="month" name="" id="">

// Define a month picker, allow user to choose one month and year.

e.g.

<form action="myFile.php"> // php file processes the inputted data

Please click the month picker to choose one month and year:

<input **type="month"** name="m" id="m">

</form>

// Output: Please click the month picker to choose one month and year:

--------- ----

<input type="number"> syntax:

<input type="number" id="" name="" min="" max="">

// Define a number field, allow user to enter a number.

e.g.

<form action="myFile.php"> // php file processes the inputted data

Enter a number between 1 and 10:

<input **type="number"** id="n" name="n" min="1" max="10">

<input type="submit">

</form>

// Output:

Enter a number between 1 and 10: Submit

<input type = “password”> syntax:

<input type = “password” id="" name= “” maxlength=””>

// Password box can be used to input password by user.

// type = “password” specifies the input type as "password"

// maxlength=”” specifies the maximum number of characters which can be entered into an input field.

e.g.

<form action="myFile.php"> // php file processes the inputted data

Your Name:

<input type = "text" name= "username">

Your Password:

<input **type = "password"** name= "password" maxlength="12">

</form>

// Output:

Your Name:

Your Password:

<input type=”radio”> syntax:

<input type=”radio” id="" name=”” value=””>

// Radio can be used to select one of the options by user.

```
// type = "radio" specifies the input type as "radio".
// Only one circle of the radio group can be selected at any time.
e.g.
<form action="myFile.php">   // php file processes the inputted data
Red <input type="radio" name="rd" value="Red">
Yellow <input type="radio" name="rd" value="Yellow">
Green <input type="radio" name="rd" value="Green">
<input  type = "submit"  name= "sbmt"  value="Submit" >
</form>
// Output:
```

<input type="range"> syntax:

```
<input type="range" id="" name="" min="" max="">
// Define a slider for entering a number within the specified range.
e.g.
<form action="myFile.php">   // php file processes the inputted data
Shift the slider between 1 to 10:<br>
<input type="range" id="n" name="n" min="1" max="10">
<input type="submit">
</form>
// Output:
Shift the slider between 1 to 10:
```

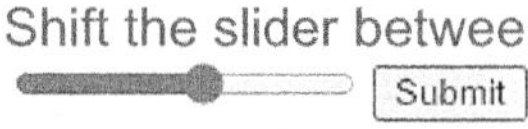

<input type = "reset"> syntax:

```
<input  type = "reset"  name= ""  value="Reset">
// Reset button can be used to reset the data that have been inputted.
// Specify the input type as "reset".
e.g.
<form action="myFile.php">   // php file processes the inputted data
Your Name: <br>
<input  type = "text"  name= "username"><br>
Your Password:<br>
<input  type = "password"  name= "password" maxlength="12">
<br><br>
<input  type = "reset"  name= "rst"  value="Reset" >
</form>
// Output:
```

<input type="search"> syntax:

```
<input type="search" id="" name="">
// Define a search field
```

e.g.
<form action="myFile.php"> // php file processes the inputted data
Search:
<input **type="search"** id="n" name="n">
<input type="submit">
</form>
// Output: Search:

<input type = "submit"> syntax:

<input type = "submit" name= "" value="">
// Submit button can be used to submit the data to process.
// type = "submit" specifies the input type as "submit".
e.g.
<form action="myFile.php"> // php file processes the inputted data
Your Name:
<input type = "text" name= "username">
Your Password:
<input type = "password" name= "password" maxlength="12">

<input **type = "submit"** name= "sbmt" value="Submit" >
</form>
// Output:

<input type="tel"> syntax:

<input type="tel" id="" name="" placeholder="xxx-xxx-xxx" pattern="[0-9]{x}-[0-9]{x}-[0-9]{x}" required>
// Define a telephone field for entering call number.
<form action="myFile.php"> // php file processes the inputted data
Please enter a telephone number:
<input type="tel" id="phone" placeholder="012-345-6789"
pattern="[0-9]{3}-[0-9]{3}-[0-9]{4}" required**>**
<input type="submit">
</form>
// Output: Please enter a telephone number:

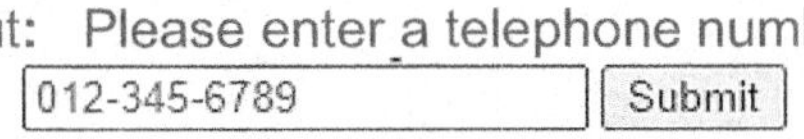

<input type = "text"> syntax:

<input type = "text" id="" name= "" value="default">
// The text box can be used to input data by user.
// Specify the input type as "text"
e.g.
<form action="myFile.php"> // php file processes the inputted data
Your Name:

```
<input  type = "text"  name= "username"><br>
Your Email:<br>
<input  type = "text"  name= "email"><br>
Your Phone: <br>
<input  type = "text"  name= "phone"><br>
</form>
// Output:
```

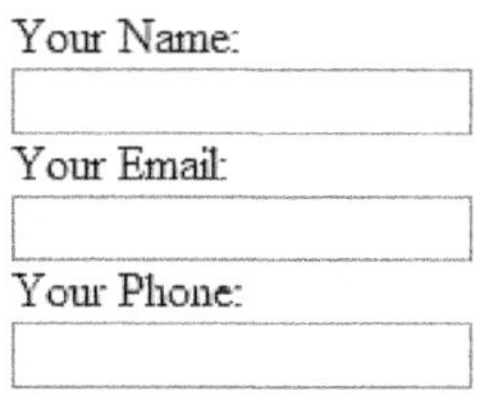

<input type="time"> syntax:

```
<input type="time" id="" name="">
// Define a time picker, allow user to select a time.
e.g.
<form action="myFile.php">   // php file processes the inputted data
Please click the time picker to select a time:<br>
<input type="time" id="t" name="t">
<input type="submit">
</form>
// Output:   Please click the time picker to select a time:
```

<input type="url"> syntax:

```
<input type="url" name="" id="">
// Define an url field which can validate the url when submitted
e.g.
<form action="myFile.php">   // php file processes the inputted data
Please enter the url:<br>
<input type="url" id="u" name="u">
<input type="submit">
</form>
// Output:   Please enter the url:
```

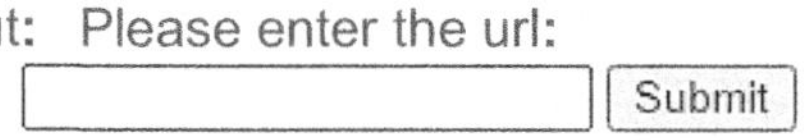

<input type="week"> syntax:

```
<input type="week" name="" id="">
// Define a week picker, allow user to choose one week.
e.g.
<form action="myFile.php">   // php file processes the inputted data
Please click the week picker to choose one week:
<input type="week" name="w" id="w">
</form>
// Output:    Please click the week picker to choose one week:
```

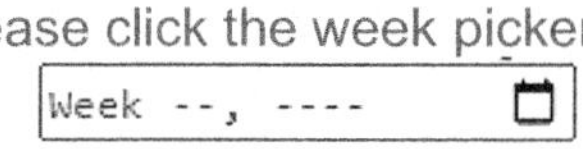

<ins> syntax:

<ins>This is an ins text. </ins>

// Show text with underline

e.g.

Note: **<ins>**This is an ins text. **</ins>**

// Output: *Note:* <ins>This is an ins text.</ins>

<label> syntax:

<label for="element_id"> text </label>

// Define a label for an element by id

e.g.

```
<form action=" ">
<input type="checkbox" id="green" value="APPLE">
  <label for="green">APPLE</label><br>
<input type="checkbox" id="yellow" value="BANANA">
  <label for="yellow">BANANA</label><br>
<input type="checkbox" id="red" value="CHERRY">
  <label for="red">CHERRY</label><br><br>
</form>
```

// Output:

☐ APPLE
☐ BANANA
☐ CHERRY

<legend> syntax:

<legend> Caption </legend>

// Define a caption and a frame for the <legend> tag.

e.g.

```
<fieldset>
 <legend>Member</legend>
  name <input type="text" id="name" name="name"><br><br>
  age <input type="text" id="age" name="age"><br><br>
  email <input type="email" id="email" name="email"><br>
</fieldset>
```

// Output:

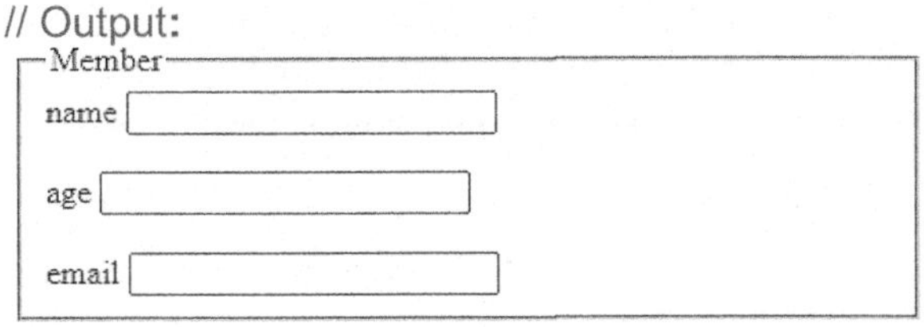

<li> syntax:

<li>List item content</li>

// Define a list item. It is typically used within either an ordered list (<ol>) or an unordered list (<ul>).

e.g.

```
<body>
  <ul>
    <li>The 1st item</li>
```

<li>The 2nd item</li>
<li>The 3rd item</li>
</ul>
</body>
// Output:

- The 1st item
- The 2nd item
- The 3rd item

<kbd> syntax:

<kbd> key </kbd>
// Define a key of the keyboard as input
e.g.
<kbd>Ctrl</kbd> + **<kbd>C</kbd>** can copy text
<kbd>Ctrl</kbd> + **<kbd>V</kbd>** can paste text
// Output:
Ctrl + C can copy text
Ctrl + V can paste text

<line> syntax:

<line x1="" y1="" x2="" y2="" stroke="" stroke-width=""/>
// Create a line in svg.
// "x1" is the x-coordinate of the line's starting point.
// "y1" is the y-coordinate of the line's starting point.
// "x2" is the x-coordinate of the line's ending point.
// "y2" is the y-coordinate of the line's ending point.
// "stroke": line color. "stroke-width": line color width.
e.g.
<svg height="200" width="200">
<**line** x1="0" y1="0" x2="100" y2="50" stroke="red" stroke-width="3"/>
</svg>

// Output: 

<link> syntax:

<link rel = "stylesheet" type = "text/css" title = "" href = "file" >
// Link an external css file to the current html document.
e.g.
(1) myStyle.css // this is an external css file
p {color: purple; background: yellow} // set yellow background
(2) myFile.html // this is an html document
<html>
<link rel = "stylesheet" type = "text/css" href = "myStyle.css" >
<p>This is an HTML file.</p>
</html>
// Output:
This is an HTML file.

<main> syntax:

<main> text </main>

// Specify the main part of the document.

e.g.

```
<article>
<i>I usually speak Cantonese language</i>
<main>
  <h3>About Cantonese Language</h3>
  <p>Cantonese is a language with a history of thousands of years, it is
spoken in Canton, Hong Kong, Macau, and Southern area of China.</p>
</main>
</article>
```

// Output:

I usually speak Cantonese language

About Cantonese Language

Cantonese is a language with a history of thousands of years, it is spoken in Canton, Hong Kong, Macau, and Southern area of China.

<map> syntax:

```
<img src=" " width="" height="" usemap="#mapName"/>
<map name="mapName">
<area shape="" coords="" href="" alt="">
</map>
```

// <map> defines an image map which contains the <area> elements.

// <area> defines a clickable area inside the <map> element, the <area> can redirect a page to another specified page.

// "usemap" specifies that the image is applied to <map> by map name.

// "shape" specifies the shape of the area.

// "coords" specifies the coordinates of an area in an image map.

// "href" sets the url of the page. "alt" sets an alternate text.

e.g.

```
<img src="pic.jpg" width="300" height="120" usemap="#myMap"/>
  <map name="myMap">
    <area shape="poly"  coords="59,31,28,83,91,83"
            href="c#.htm"  alt="poly">
    <area shape="circle"  coords="155,56,26"
            href="ruby.htm"  alt="circle">
    <area shape="rect"  coords="224,30,276,82"
            href="java.htm"  alt="rectangle">
  </map>
```

// Output:

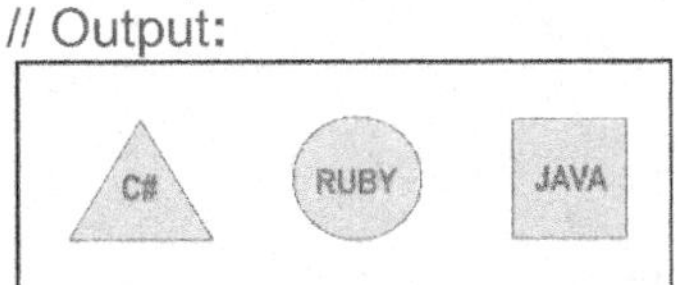

// Assume that we click the triangle(c#) area, it will redirect the page to the c#.html page.

<mark> syntax:

<mark> text </mark>

// Highlight the specified text to yellow.

e.g.
<p>Please attend **<mark>the meeting</mark>** on time!</p>
// Output:
Please attend the meeting on time!

<marquee> syntax:

<marquee direction="" scrollamount="" height="" width="" >
Scrolling Text
</marquee>
// Scroll the text up or down, left or right.
// "direction=value" specifies the direction of the scroll. (Value as up, down, left or right.)
// "scrollamount=value" specifies the speed to scroll.(Value as 2-10)
"height" and "width" specifies the size to scrolling texts.
e.g.
<marquee direction=left scrollamount=5 height=50 width=500>
This is the scrolling text, the scrolling direction is left, the scrolling amount is 5, the text height is 50, and the text width is 500.......
</marquee>
// Output:

<<< This is the scrolling text, the scro

<meta> syntax:

<meta name = "" content = "">
// <meta> is used to declare some information, such as http-equiv, description, keywords, author, ISBN……
e.g.
<head>
<**meta** name = "keywords" content = "red, yellow, green">
<**meta** name = "description" content = "Colors">
<**meta** name = "author" content = "Ray Yao">
<**meta** name = "ISBN" content = "0-123456-789">
</head>
// "keywords" are used to specify keywords for search engines.
// "description" is used to provide content for search engines.
// "ISBN" is a unique numeric commercial book identifier.

<meter> syntax:

<meter id=" " value="fraction">percentage</meter>
// Define a graphic representation of a fractional number.
e.g.
<label for="A">Support Rate of Candidate A:</label>
<meter id="A" value="0.3">30%</meter>
<label for="B">Support Rate of Candidate B:</label>
<meter id="B" value="0.7">70%</meter>
// Output:
Support Rate of Candidate A:
Support Rate of Candidate B:

<nav> syntax:

```
<nav> <a href="url"</a> </nav>
// Define a set of navigation hyperlinks
e.g.
<nav>
 <a href="https://www.yahoo.com">Yahoo</a> |
 <a href="https://www.google.com">Google</a> |
 <a href="https://www.amazon.com">Amazon</a> |
</nav>
// Output:   Yahoo | Google | Amazon |
```

<noscript> syntax:

```
<noscript> text </noscript>
// Show the text if the browser does not support the current script.
e.g.
<script>
document.write("Your browser support JavaScript!")
</script>
<noscript>
Note: your browser does not support JavaScript!
</noscript>   // assume that your browser does not support js.
// Output:
Note: your browser does not support JavaScript!
```

<object> syntax:

```
<object data = "" type = "" width = "" height = ""> </object>
// Embed all kinds of resources into the html document.
// "data" attribute specifies the resource url, it can be an image, a file...
// "type" attribute specifies the MIME type of the resource.
e.g.(1)
<object data="flower.jpg" type="image/jpeg" width="100" height="100">
</object>
// Output:
```

```
e.g. (2)
<object data="myDoc.html" type="text/html" width="300" height="200">
</object>
```

// Output: *Hello, I am an html file; I am embedded in the current HTML document. You are able to see me now!*

<ol> and <li>syntax:

```
<ol type = "style">
<li>……</li>
</ol>
```

// <ol> sets ordered lists. type = "1" sets sequence numbers. type = "A" sets sequence uppercase letter A,B,C.... type = "a" sets sequence lowercase letter a,b,c......

e.g.

```
<ol type = "1">
<li>AAAAA</li>
<li>BBBBB</li>
<li>CCCCC</li>
</ol>
// Output:
    1.  AAAAA
    2.  BBBBB
    3.  CCCCC
```

```
<ol type = "A">
<li>AAAAA</li>
<li>BBBBB</li>
<li>CCCCC</li>
</ol>
// Output:
    A.  AAAAA
    B.  BBBBB
    C.  CCCCC
```

```
<ol type = "a">
<li>AAAAA</li>
<li>BBBBB</li>
<li>CCCCC</li>
</ol>
// Output:
    a.  AAAAA
    b.  BBBBB
    c.  CCCCC
```

<optgroup> syntax:

```
<optgroup label="">
   <option value=""> text </option>
</optgroup>
// Group associated options into one <select> element.
e.g.
<select  name="Books" id="Books">
  <optgroup label="Cheat Sheet">
    <option value="C#">C# Cheat Sheet</option>
    <option value="C++">C++ Cheat Sheet</option>
  </optgroup>
  <optgroup label="In 8 Hours">
    <option value="R">R in 8 Hours</option>
    <option value="LUA">LUA in 8 Hours</option>
  </optgroup>
</select>
// Output:
```

C# Cheat Sheet

<option> syntax:

```
<select  name="">
    <option value="">...</option>
    <option value="">...</option>
</select>
// <select> tag is used to create a drop-down list.
// <option> tag contains the value for user to choose.
e.g.
<form action="myFile.php">
<select  name="mySelect">
   <option value="apple">Apple</option>
   <option value="banana">Banana</option>
   <option value="cherry">Cherry</option>
</select>
<input  type="submit"  value="Submit">
</form>
```

// Output:

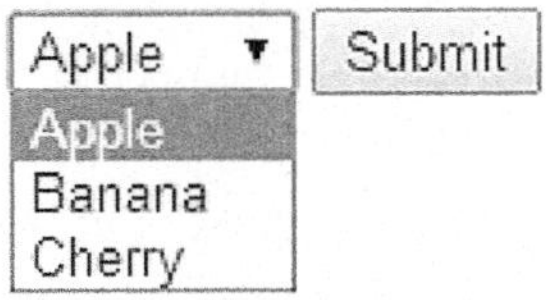

<output> syntax:

<form oninput = "result = expression">
// Calculate the expression, "oninput" passes result to <output> tag.
<output id=""></output>
// Show the result of calculation.
e.g.

```
<form oninput="sum.value=parseInt(x.value)+parseInt(y.value);">
 <input type="number" id="x" value=""/><br>
 + <br/>
 <input type="number" id="y" value=""/><br>
 = <br>
 Result: <output id="sum"></output>
</form>
```

// Output:

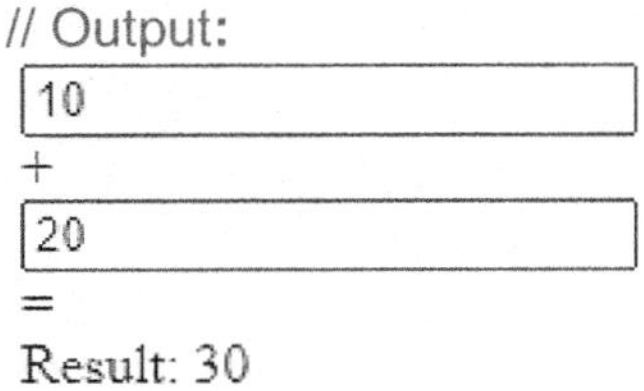

<p> syntax:

<p> paragraph </p>
// Separate the texts, and leaves an empty line between each paragraph.
e.g.

```
<p>This is the first paragraph. Hi, how are you? Do you like HTML, it is fantastic! </p> <p>This is the second paragraph. Hello, how are you doing? I am learning HTML, it is interesting! </p>
```

// Output:
This is the first paragraph. Hi, how are you? Do you like HTML, it is fantastic!
This is the second paragraph. Hello, how are you doing? I am learning HTML, it is interesting!

<param> syntax:

<param name="" value="">
// Set parameters for <object> element
// Note: The <param> tag is not supported in html5.
e.g.

```
<object data="myMusic.mp3">
  <param name="audio" value="play">
</object>
```

// Output:

<path> syntax:

<path d="x1,y1 x2,y2 x3,y3 Z" fill="color"/>
// Create a path in svg.
// "x1" is the x-coordinate of the path's starting point.
// "y1" is the y-coordinate of the path's starting point.
// "x2" is the x-coordinate of the path's ending point and next path's starting point.
// "y2" is the y-coordinate of the path's ending point and next path's starting point.

M	move to
L	line to
H	horizontal line to
V	vertical line to
C	curve to
S	smooth curve to
Q	quadratic bézier curve
T	smooth quadratic bézier curve to
A	elliptical arc
Z	close path

e.g.
<svg height="200" width="200">
<**path** d="M80,0 L0,100 L160,100 Z" fill="green"/>
</svg> // M80,0 means the starting point of path is (80,0)

// Output: 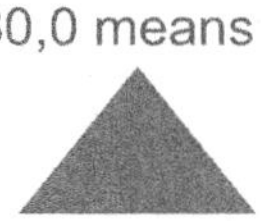

<picture> syntax:

<picture>
<source media="..." srcset="...">
<source media="..." srcset="...">
<img src="...">
</picture>
// <picture> element is a container for two <source> elements and one <img> element. It allows to specify several images designed to better fill the browser viewport properly.
// The browser always displays the first <source> element whose image matches the current viewport width.
// "media" specifies the minimum width of the images.
// "srcset" and "img" specifies the different images
e.g.
<picture>
<source media="(min-width:500px)" srcset="flower1.jpg">
<source media="(min-width:700px)" srcset="flower2.jpg">
<img src="flowers3.jpg" alt="Flowers" style="width:auto;">
</picture>
// Output:

<polygon> syntax:

<polygon points="x1,y1 x2,y2 x3,y3..." stroke="" stroke-width="" fill=""/>

// Create a polygon in svg.
// "x1,y1 x2,y2 x3,y3" sets x and y coordinates of each polygon corner.
// "stroke":polygon line. "stroke-width":polygon line width. "fill":fills color
e.g.

```
<svg width="200" height="150">
 <polygon points="50,5  20,99  96,39  5,38  80,99"
 stroke="green" stroke-width="3" fill="green"/>
</svg>
```

// Output: 

<polyline> syntax:

<polyline points="x1,y1 x2,y2 x3,y3..." stroke="" stroke-width="" fill=""/>

// Create a polyline in svg.
// "x1,y1 x2,y2 x3,y3" sets x and y coordinates of each line point.
// "stroke":polyline line. "stroke-width":polyline line width "fill": fills color
e.g.

```
<svg width="200" height="150">
 <polyline points="0,30  20,0  40,30  60,0  80,30  100,0"
 stroke="green" stroke-width="1" fill="none"/>
</svg>
```

// Output: 

<pre> syntax:

<pre> text </pre>

// Retain the pre-formatted text, it can preserve the original white space, tabs, line breaks, fixed–width font
e.g.

```
<pre>
  ------------------------------
\       @     @       /
  \         v         /
        ------------------
</pre>
```

// Output:

```
 ------------------------------
\       @     @       /
  \         v         /
        ------------------
```

// Note: If we don't use <pre> tags, the output will be:

```
 --------------- \ @ @ / \ v / -----------
```

<progress> syntax:

<progress id=" " value="" max=""> percentage </progress>

// Display the progress of a task. "value" specifies how much task have been completed. "max" specifies how much task totally.

// Note: <progress> has no "min", but minimum value is 0 by default.

e.g.

<label for="app">Installing progress:</label>

<progress id="app" value="0.70" max="1"> 70% **</progress>**

// Output:

Installing progress: 

<q> syntax:

<q> text </q>

// Define a short quotation.

e.g.

<p>About Ray Yao's website, it says: **<q>**We sell both Paperbacks and Kindle books, the searching keywords are: Xxxxxx by Ray Yao**</q>**</p>

// Output:

About Ray Yao's website, it says: We sell both Paperbacks and Kindle books, the searching keywords are: Xxxxxx by Ray Yao

---

<rect> syntax:

<rect width="" height="" stroke="" stroke-width="" fill="color"/>

// Create a rectangle in svg.

// "stroke": rectangle border. "stroke-width": rectangle border width

e.g.

<svg width="200" height="100">

<**rect** width="180" height="80" stroke="red" stroke-width="3" fill="yellow"/>

</svg>

// Output: 

<rp> syntax:

<ruby>

East_Asian_Text <rp>(</rp> <rt> annotation </rt> <rp>)</rp>

</ruby>

// Define the content to be shown in the browser that does not support ruby annotations.

e.g.

<ruby>

朋友 **<rp>(</rp>** <rt> friends </rt> **<rp>)</rp>**

</ruby> // assume that my browser supports the ruby annotations

// Output:

friends
朋友

<ruby> <rt> syntax:

<ruby>

East_Asian_Text <rt> annotation </rt>
</ruby>
// Define an annotation on the top of the East Asian Text.
e.g.
<ruby>
朋友 **<rt>** friends **</rt>**
</ruby>
// Output:
friends
朋友

<s> syntax:

<s> text </s>
// Specify the text no longer correct or accurate. The text middle will have a deleting line.
e.g.
<s>The salary is $10000.</s> <i>The salary is $20000 now.</i>
// Output: ~~The salary is $10000.~~ *The salary is $20000 now.*

<samp> syntax:

<samp> text </samp>
// Display the sample output from a computer program or a script.
e.g.
<p>I am running a program but it shows a message:</p>
<samp>Error: Access is denied.**</samp>**
// Output:
I am running a program but it shows a message
`Error: Access is denied.`

<script> syntax:

<script> text </script>
// <script> element is used to embed executable code or script.
e.g.
<script>
document.write("Your browser support JavaScript!")
</script>
// Output:
Your browser support JavaScript!

<section> syntax:

<section> text <section>
// Create standalone sections in a document containing related contents
e.g.
<section>
<h3>PHP</h3> PHP is a popular open source programming language· PHP program can be executed on the server.
</section>
<section>
<h3>MySQL</h3> MySQL is the world's most widely-used open source database.

```
</section>
```

// Output:

PHP

PHP is a popular open source programming language· PHP program can be executed on the server.

MySQL

MySQL is the world's most widely-used open source database.

<select> <option> syntax:

```
<select  name="">
   <option value="">...</option>
   <option value="">...</option>
</select>
```

// <select> tag is used to create a drop-down list.
// <option> tag contains the value for user to choose.

e.g.

```
<form action="myFile.php">
<select  name="mySelect">
   <option value="apple">Apple</option>
   <option value="banana">Banana</option>
   <option value="cherry">Cherry</option>
</select>
<input  type="submit"  value="Submit">
</form>
```

// Output:

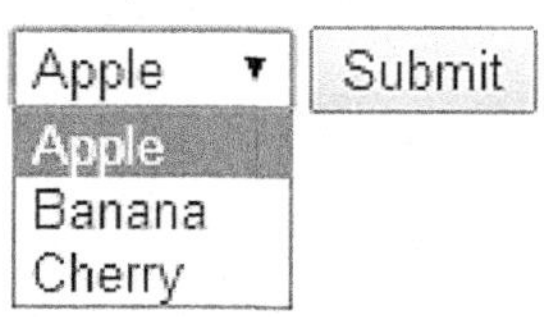

<slot> syntax:

```
<slot></slot>
```

// A placeholder for rendering content in web components.

e.g.

```
<!DOCTYPE html>
<html lang="en">
<body>
   <custom-tag>
      <span>Slot content here!</span>
   </custom-tag>
   <script>
      class MyTag extends HTMLElement {
         constructor() {
            super();
            this.attachShadow({ mode: 'open' }).innerHTML = ``;
               <slot></slot>
         }}
      customElements.define('custom-tag', MyTag);
   </script>
```

</body>
</html>
// Output: Slot content here!

<small> syntax:

<small>This is a small text. </small>
// Show text in a small font
e.g.
Note: **<small>**This is a small text. **</small>**
// Output: *Note:* **This is a small text.**

<source> syntax:

<source src="" type="">   or   <source media="" srcset="">
// Specify multiple media resources for media elements, such as <audio>, <video>, and <picture>.
e.g.
<audio controls>
<**source** src="myMusic.mp3" type="audio/mpeg">
</audio>
<video controls>
<**source** src="myMovie.mp4" type="video/mp4">
</video>
<picture>
<**source** media="(min-width:500px)" srcset="flower.jpg">
</picture>
// Output:

<span> syntax:

<span class = "value"> text </span>
<span id = "value"> text </span>
// Define a specified style for part of a text, of part of a document
// <span> can be used as inline tag. <div> can be used as block tag.
e.g.
<style type = "text/css">
.d1{font-style: italic;color: purple;}
#d2{font-family: arial black;color: blue;}
</style>
This is **<span** class = "d1"> AAA text **</span>**
This is **<span** id = "d2"> BBB text **</span>**
// Output: This is *AAA text*   This is **BBB text**

<strike> syntax:

// <strike> tag does not support html5.
// <strike> tag is same as <del> tag; please see <del> tag.

<strong> syntax:

<strong>This is a strong text. </strong>

// Show text in a bold font
e.g.
Note: **<strong>**This is a strong text. **</strong>**
// Output: *Note:* **This is a strong text.**

<style> of class syntax:

<style type = "text/css"> .class{attribute:value} </style>
// Define a class style css
// Apply the specified style to the class and its content.
e.g.
<style type = "text/css">
.a {color: blue}
.b {font-style: italic}
</style>
<h3 **class = "a"**> Hello Css </h3>
<p **class = "b"**> Test Class Style Css </p>
// Output: Hello Css *Test Class Style Css*

<style> of id syntax:

<style type = "text/css"> #id{attribute:value} </style>
// Define an id style css
// Apply the specified style to the id and its content.
e.g.
<style type = "text/css">
#a {color: blue}
#b {font-style: italic}
</style>
<h3 **id = "a"**> Hello Css </h3>
<p **id = "b"**> Test Id Style Css </p>

// Output: Hello Css *Test Id Style Css*

<style> of tap syntax:

<style type = "text/css"> tap{attribute:value} </style>
// Define a tag style css
// Apply the specified style to the tag and its content.
e.g.
<style type = "text/css">
h4 {color: blue}
p {font-style: italic}
</style>
<h4>Hello Css**</h4>**
<p>Test Tag Style Css**</p>**
// Output: Hello Css *Test Tag Style Css*

<sub> syntax:

_{text}
// Show subscript text
e.g.
Water is H **_{** 2 **}** O.

// Output: Water is H_2O.

<summary> syntax:

<summary> clickable_heading </summary>
// Define a heading for <details> element. The heading can be clickable for view/hide the contents.
e.g.
<details>
<summary>About Cantonese Language</summary>
<p>Cantonese is a language with a history of thousands of years, it is spoken in Canton, Hong Kong, Macau, and Southern area of China.</p>
</details>

// Output: ▼ About Cantonese Language

Cantonese is a language with a history of thousands of years, it is spoken in Canton, Hong Kong, Macau, and Southern area of China.

<sup> syntax:

^{text}
// Show superscript text
e.g.
2 **^{** 3 **}** = 8
// Output: $2^3 = 8$

<svg> syntax:

<svg width="" height=""> graphic_element </svg>
// Create a container for SVG graphics.
// SVG graphics refer to boxes, circles, triangle, rectangle……
// To know more SVG, please reference some related SVG books.
e.g.
<svg width="200" height="50">
<rect width="200" height="50" style="fill:green" />
</svg>
// Output:

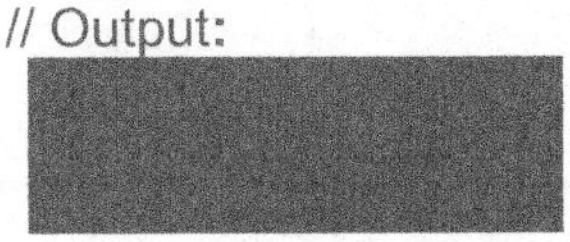

<table>, <tr>, <td> syntax:

<table border="" bordercolor="" width="" height="" bgcolor="" cellspacing="">
<tr>
<td> </td>
</tr>
</table>
// <table border = value></table> creates a table with borders.
// "bgcolor" sets background color, "bordercolor" sets border color.
// "width" sets width of table, "height" sets height of table
// "cellspacing" sets cell spaces.

```
// <tr></tr> is row tags.  <td></td> is cell tags.
e.g.
<table border = "1" bgcolor = "yellow" bordercolor="red" >
<tr>
<td>Cell 1</td>
<td>Cell 2</td>
<td>Cell 3</td>
</tr>
<tr>
<td>Cell 4</td>
<td>Cell 5</td>
<td>Cell 6</td>
</tr>
</table>
// Output:
```

Cell 1	Cell 2	Cell 3
Cell 4	Cell 5	Cell 6

<tbody> syntax:

```
<tbody>
<tr>  <td>text1</td>   <td>text2</td>   <td>text3</td>  </tr>
</tbody>
// Define the body of a table
e.g.
<table>
  <thead>
    <tr><th>Books</th><th>Price</th></tr>
  </thead>
  <tbody>
    <tr><td>Java</td><td>$100</td></tr>
    <tr><td>Html</td><td>$100</td></tr>
    <tr><td>Ruby</td><td>$100</td></tr>
  </tbody>
  <tfoot>
    <tr><td>Sum</td><td>$300</td></tr>
  </tfoot>
</table>
// Output:
```

Books	Price
Java	$100
Html	$100
Ruby	$100
Sum	$300

<td> syntax:

```
<td width="" rowspan="" colspan="">
// "width" sets the width of a cell
```

// "rowspan" sets the numbers of rows to span across.
// "colspan" sets the numbers of column to span across.

e.g.

```
<table border = "1" >
<tr>
<td width=100 rowspan = 2>Cell 1</td>
<td>Cell 2</td><td>Cell 3</td>
</tr>
<tr>
<td>Cell 5</td><td>Cell 6</td>
</tr>
</table>
```

// Output:

Cell 1	Cell 2	Cell 3
	Cell 5	Cell 6

<template> syntax:

<template> contents </template>

// Create a container holding some contents hidden from users.
// <template> usually works with JavaScript to show the hidden contents in the template.

e.g.

```
<template>
  <p><img src="flower.jpg" width="100" height="100"></p>
</template>
<button onclick="show()">View Template Contents</button>
<script>   // When the button is clicked, the show() will be executed
function show() {
  var temp = document.getElementsByTagName("template")[0];
  // Access the contents in the first template
  var fl = temp.content.cloneNode(true);
  // clone the contents in the template to the variable "fl"
  document.body.appendChild(fl);
  // show the "fl" value
}
</script>
```

// Output:

View Template Contents

<text> syntax:

<text x="" y="" fill="color" transform="rotate(angle)"> </text>

// Define a text in svg
// "x" is the x-coordinate of the text starting point
// "y" is the y-coordinate of the text starting point

// "rotate(angle)" specifies the angle the text will rotate.
e.g.
```
<svg width="100" height="100" >
<text x="20" y="20" fill="blue" transform="rotate(30)">Hello World!</text>
</svg>
```
// Output: *Hello World!*

<textarea> syntax:

<textarea name="" rows="" cols="">......</textarea>

// <textarea> can be used to input multi-line text by user.
// The <textarea> specifies the input type as "text area", which is used to input multi-line.
e.g.
```
<form>
<textarea name="ta" rows="3" cols="28">
Hello! Here is textarea.
</textarea>
</form>
```
// Output:

```
Hello! Here is textarea.
```

<tfoot> syntax:

```
<tfoot>
<tr> <td>text1</td> <td>text2</td> <td>text3</td> </tr>
</tfoot>
```
// Define the footer of a table
e.g.
```
<table>
 <thead>
  <tr><th>Books</th><th>Price</th></tr>
 </thead>
 <tbody>
  <tr><td>Java</td><td>$100</td></tr>
  <tr><td>Html</td><td>$100</td></tr>
  <tr><td>Ruby</td><td>$100</td></tr>
 </tbody>
 <tfoot>
  <tr><td>Sum</td><td>$300</td></tr>
 </tfoot>
</table>
```
// Output:

Books	Price
Java	$100
Html	$100
Ruby	$100

Books	Price
Sum	$300

<th> syntax:

```
<tr>  <th>text1</th>  <th>text2</th>  <th>text3</th>  </tr>
```

// Define a header cell in a table, it contain the table headings.

e.g.

```
<table>
<tr><th>Books</th><th>Price</th></tr>
<tr><td>Java</td><td>$100</td></tr>
<tr><td>Html</td><td>$100</td></tr>
<tr><td>Ruby</td><td>$100</td></tr>
<tr><td>Sum</td><td>$300</td></tr>
</table>
```

// Output:

Books	Price
Java	$100
Html	$100
Ruby	$100
Sum	$300

<thead> syntax:

```
 <thead>
 <tr>  <th>text1</th>  <th>text2</th>  <th>text3</th>  </tr>
 </thead>
```

// Define the header of a table

e.g.

```
<table>
 <thead>
  <tr><th>Books</th><th>Price</th></tr>
 </thead>
 <tbody>
  <tr><td>Java</td><td>$100</td></tr>
  <tr><td>Html</td><td>$100</td></tr>
  <tr><td>Ruby</td><td>$100</td></tr>
 </tbody>
 <tfoot>
  <tr><td>Sum</td><td>$300</td></tr>
 </tfoot>
</table>
```

// Output:

Books	Price
Java	$100
Html	$100
Ruby	$100
Sum	$300

<time> syntax:

```
<time datetime=""> text </time>     // define a datetime
<time> time </time>     // define a time (24-hours clock)
e.g.
<time datetime="2023-01-01 00:00">New Year's Day</time>
Office Hours: <time>09:00</time> -- <time>17:00</time>
// Output:    New Year's Day     Office Hours: 09:00 -- 17:00
```

<title> syntax:

```
<title> text </title>
// Define a title of a document.
e.g.
<html>
<head>    // <title> always locates in between <head></head>.
  <title> C++ Cheat Sheet </title>
</head>
<body>
</body>
</html>
// Output:   C++ Cheat Sheet
```

<tr> syntax:

```
<tr align="" valign="" height = num>
// "align=value" sets the text on left, center, right inside a cell.
// "valign=value" sets the text on top, middle, bottom inside a cell.
// "height=num" sets the height of the row.
e.g.
<table border = "1" width = 200 height = 100 >
<tr align = center  valign = middle   height = 50>
<td>Cell 1</td>
<td>Cell 2</td>
<td>Cell 3</td>
</tr>
</table>
// Output:
```

Cell 1	Cell 2	Cell 3

<track> syntax:

```
<track src="" kind="" srclang="" label="" default>
// Define subtitle, caption, description for <audio> or <video> element.
// "src" specifies a track file. "kind" sets the subtitle, caption…
// "kind" specifies the kind of text track.
// "srclang" sets the language. "label" sets the title of the text track.
// "default" sets the track enabled unless user sets other preferences.
e.g.
<video controls="controls">
<source src="myVideo.mp4" type="video/mp4">
```

<track src="myTrack.vtt" kind="subtitles" srclang="en" default>
</video>
// Here is the content of the track file (myTrack.vtt):

```
WEBVTT
00:00:00.000 --> 00:00:10.000
This is the first content of myTrack.vtt file
00:00:10.000 --> 00:00:20.000
This is the second content of myTrack.vtt file
00:00:20.000 --> 00:00:30.000
This is the third content of myTrack.vtt file
```

<u> syntax:

<u> text </u>
// Underline the unarticulated text or different style text.
e.g.
<p>We are using **<u>the <u> tag</u>** as an example</p>
// Output: We are using the <u> tag as an example

<ul> and <li>syntax:

<ul type = "style">
<li>……</li>
</ul>
// <ul> sets unordered lists.
// type = "disc" sets a solid disc.
// type = "circle" sets an empty circle.
// type = "square" sets a solid square.
e.g.

<ul type = "disc">
<li>AAAAA</li>
<li>BBBBB</li>
<li>CCCCC</li>
</ul>
// Output:

- AAAAA
- BBBBB
- CCCCC

<ul type = "circle">
<li>AAAAA</li>
<li>BBBBB</li>
<li>CCCCC</li>
</ul>
// Output:

○ AAAAA
○ BBBBB
○ CCCCC

<ul type = "square">
<li>AAAAA</li>
<li>BBBBB</li>
<li>CCCCC</li>
</ul>
// Output:

▪ AAAAA
▪ BBBBB
▪ CCCCC

<var> syntax:

<var> variable </var>
// Define a variable in programming
e.g.
<p>Equations: **<var>x</var>** + **<var>y</var>** = 100</p>
// Output: Equations: x + y = 100

<video controls> syntax:

<video width="" height="" controls>
<source src="video_file" type="video/mp4">

</video>
// Embed a video control to the current page.
e.g.
<video width="300" height="200" controls>
<source src="myMovie.mp4" type="video/mp4">
</video>
// Output:

<wbr> syntax:

text<wbr>text<wbr>text<wbr>text.....
// Specify a word break opportunity within a very long word. A long word may be like this: aequeosalinocalcalinoceraceoaluminosocupreovitriolic.
// Without <wbr>, it is a little difficult to read a very long word.
//
 forces a break while <wbr> only means a break opportunity.
e.g.
An original long word: <i>Counterclockwise</i>
Using the <wbr> tags: <i>Counter**<wbr>**clock**<wbr>**wise</i>
// Output:
An original long word: *Counterclockwise*
Using the <wbr> tags: *Counterclockwise*

---

accept syntax:

<input accept="type">
// Specify the file type that the server only accept.
// The "type" can be image/*, audio/*, video/*, gif, .jpg, .png, .doc.
e.g.
<form action="myFile.php">
Please select an image:
<input type="file" id="img" **accept="image/*"**>
<input type="submit">
// Output: Please select an image:

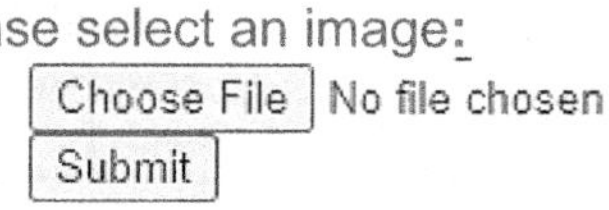

---

accept-charset syntax:

<form accept-charset="character_set">
// Specify the character encoding that is used for form submitting.
// "charcter_set" such as: ISO-8859-1, US-ASCII, UTF-8, GB2312...
e.g.
<form action="myFile.php" **accept-charset="UTF-8"**>
Name:<input type="text" name="n">
<input type="submit" >
</form>
// Output:

---

accesskey syntax:

accesskey="letter"
// Specifies a shortcut key to activate an element.
// Different OS and browser uses different accesskey.
// Chrome in Window and Linux uses: **Alt + accesskey**,
e.g.
<a href="https://www.yahoo.com" **accesskey="y"**>Yahoo</a>
// Output: Yahoo
// When we press **Alt + y** keys, web page will be redirected to Yahoo.

---

action syntax:

<form action="myFile.php" method="get/post">
// Specify myFile.php to process the inputted data from user.
// We can also use myFile.asp, myFile.jsp to process the inputted data.
// "get" method sends data to the server openly, small quantity.
// "post" method sends data to the server secretly, more quantity.
// To learn more how to process data, Please see *PHP Cheat Sheet.*
e.g.
<form **action="myFile.php"** method="post">
name: <input type="text" name="n">
<input type="submit">
</form>
// Output:
name: [ ] Submit

---

addColorStop() syntax:

gradient.addColorStop(offset, "color")
// Specify the offset and color of a gradient object.

offset	"0" means the start of gradient, "1" means the end of gradient
color	a css color value to be shown at the offset position

e.g.
<canvas id="cid" width="200" height="100"></canvas>
<script>
var context = cid.getContext("2d");
var gradient = context.createLinearGradient(0, 0, 200, 100);
gradient.addColorStop(0, "green"); // set offset and color
gradient.addColorStop(1, "white"); // set offset and color
context.fillStyle = gradient;
context.fillRect(10, 5, 180, 90);
</script>
// Output:

---

alt syntax:

<img src="" alt="text">
<area shape="" coords="" alt="text">
// Specify to show an alternate text if the original contents fails to show.

e.g.
<img src="flower.jpg" **alt="This is a flower"** width="90" height="60">
// Output: This is a flower

---

anchor syntax:

<a name = "xxx"> anchor </a> // set an anchor
<a href = "#xxx"> go to anchor </a> // link to the anchor
// If an article has long line contents, you need to set up some Anchors for the article so that the readers can easily jump to the content they like to read.
e.g.
<p> **<a name = "top">**This is the top **</a>** </p>
<p>Here is a long long text...... </p>
<p> **<a href = "#top">** Back to Top **</a>** </p>
// Output:
This is the top
Here is a long long text......
Back to Top

---

arc() syntax:

context.arc(x, y, r, startAngle, endAngle, counterclockwise);
// Draw a circular arc.
// "x" is the x-coordinate of the center of the circle
// "y" is the y-coordinate of the center of the circle
// "r" is the radius of the circle
// "startAngle" is the starting angle in radians
// "endAngle" is the ending angle in radians
// "counterclockwise" is optional.
e.g.
<canvas id="cid" width="100" height="50" ></canvas>
<script>
var context = cid.getContext("2d");
context.beginPath();
context.arc(50, 25, 20, 0, 2 * Math.PI);
context.stroke();
</script>

// Output: 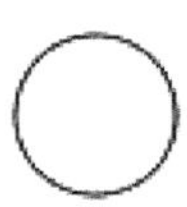

---

async syntax:

<script src="external.js" async></script>
// Specify an external script that is executed asynchronously.
e.g.
<script src="helloworld.js" **async**></script>
// Given the contents of "helloworld.js" is: alert("Hello World!");
// Output: Hello World!

---

autocomplete syntax:

<form action="" method="" autocomplete="on/off">
<input type="" id="" name="" autocomplete="on/off">

```
// Specify the autocomplete on or off for a form or an input field.
e.g.
<form action="myFile.php" method="post" autocomplete="on">
Name: <input type="text" id="n" name="n"
// Output:
```

Name: [ ] Submit

---

autofocus syntax:

```
<input type="" id="" name="" autofocus>
<textarea autofocus> text </textarea>
<button type="button" autofocus>Click Me</button>
// Specify automatic focus for <input>, <textarea>, and <button>.
e.g.
<form action="myFile.php">
Name: <input type="text" name="n" autofocus>
<input type="submit">
</form>
// Output:
```

Name: [|] Submit

---

autoplay syntax:

```
<audio controls autoplay>
<video controls autoplay>
// Specify automatic play for <audio> or <video> element.
e.g.
<video controls autoplay>
<source src="myVideo.mp4" type="video/mp4">
</video>
// Output:
```

---

beginPath() syntax:

```
context.beginPath();
// Start a path, or reset a current path
e.g.
<canvas id="cid" width="100" height="50" ></canvas>
<script>
var context = document.getElementById("cid").getContext("2d");
context.beginPath();    // Begin the line
context.moveTo(0, 0);
context.lineTo(100, 50);
context.closePath();    // Close the line
context.stroke();
</script>
```

// Output:

----

border color syntax:

border-color: value

// Set the border color

e.g.

```
<style type = "text/css">
#b5{border-style: groove; border-width: 20px; border-color: blue}
#b6{border-style: ridge; border-width: 20px; border-color: purple}
</style>
<p id = "b5">This is groove border.</p>
<p id = "b6">This is ridge border.</p
```

// Output:

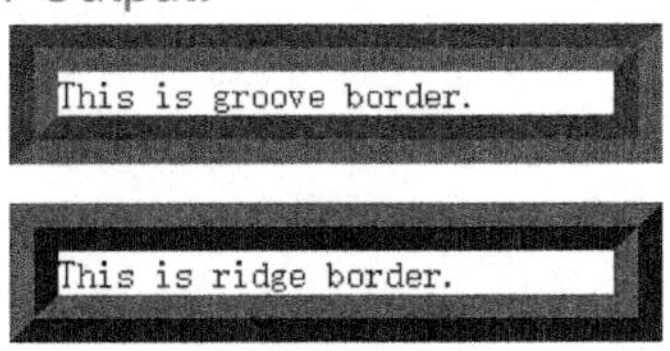

----

border style syntax:

border-style: value

// "border-style: value" can set the border style by specifying different value. The "value" may be one of the "solid, double, dashed, dotted, groove, ridge, inset, and outset".

e.g.

```
<style type = "text/css">
#b1{border-style: solid; border-width: 10px;}
#b2{border-style: double; border-width: 10px;}
#b3{border-style: dashed; border-width: 10px;}
#b4{border-style: dotted; border-width: 10px;}
#b5{border-style: groove; border-width: 10px;}
#b6{border-style: ridge; border-width: 10px;}
#b7{border-style: inset; border-width: 10px;}
#b8{border-style: outset; border-width: 10px;}
</style>
<body>
<p id = "b1">This is solid border.</p><br>
<p id = "b2">This is double border.</p><br>
<p id = "b3">This is dashed border.</p><br>
<p id = "b4">This is dotted border.</p><br>
<p id = "b5">This is groove border.</p><br>
<p id = "b6">This is ridge border.</p><br>
<p id = "b7">This is inset border.</p><br>
<p id = "b8">This is outset border.</p><br>
```

// Output:

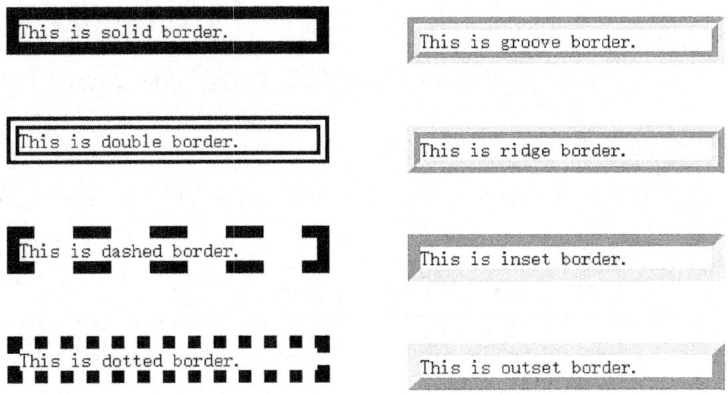

---

buffered syntax:

id.buffered.start(0) // return the start of the video buffered range
id.buffered.end(0) // return the end of the video buffered range

e.g.

```
<button onclick="fun()" type="button">Buffered Range</button><br>
<video id="vid" width="300" height="180" controls>
<source src="myVideo.mp4" type="video/mp4">
</video>
<script>
function fun() {
alert("Start: " + vid.buffered.start(0) + " End: "  + vid.buffered.end(0));
}    // (0) means the first video, if there are multiple videos in a page.
</script>
```

// Output: [Buffered Range] Start: 0 End: 59.992

---

button type syntax:

```
<input type="button" value="Click Me" onclick="alert('Clicked!')">
```

// Used with the <input> element to create a clickable button that can perform various actions, such as triggering JavaScript functions or submitting forms.

e.g.

```
<form>
  <input type="button" value="Click Me" onclick="alert('Button clicked!')">
</form>
```

// Output: [Click Me]

---

canPlayType syntax:

video_id.canPlayType("video_type")

// Check if a specific video type can be played, the result will be:

probably	probably the video can be played
maybe	maybe the video can be played
" "	sure the video cannot be played

e.g.

```
<button onclick="fun()" type="button">Can Play?</button><br>
<video id="vid" width="300" height="180" controls autoplay>
  <source  src="myVideo.mp4" type="video/mp4">
```

```
</video>
<script>
function fun(){alert("Can play? " + vid.canPlayType("video/mp4"));}
</script>
```

// Output: [Can Play?] Can play? maybe

---

charset syntax:

```
<meta charset="UTF-8">
<script src="" charset="UTF-8"></script>
```

// Specify the character encoding.
// "charcter_set" such as: ISO-8859-1, US-ASCII, UTF-8, GB2312…
e.g.

```
<head>
  <meta charset="UTF-8">
</head>
```

// Specify the "UTF-8" as the character set of the current document.

---

checkbox type syntax:

```
<input type="checkbox">
```

// Used with the <input> element to create a checkbox, which allows users to select one or more options independently.
e.g.

```
<form>
  <label for="confirm">Check to confirm:</label>
  <input type="checkbox" id="confirm" name="confirm">
</form>
```

// Output: Check to confirm: ☐

---

checked syntax:

```
<input type="checkbox" name="" value="" checked>
<input type="radio" name="" value="" checked>
```

// Define a pre-checked option for "checkbox" or "radio" input type.
e.g.

```
<form action="myFile.php">
<input type="checkbox" name="ch" value="A"> Plan A.
<input type="checkbox" name="ch" value="B" checked> Plan B.<br>
<input type="submit" value="Submit">    // "B" is pre-checked
</form>
```

// Output:

☐ Plan A. ☑ Plan B.
[Submit]

---

cite syntax:

```
<blockquote cite="url">    // specify a url where the quote is from
<ins cite="file">text</ins>  // specify a file to explain why insert text
<del cite="file">text</del>  // specify a file to explain why delete text
```

e.g.

```
<p>Here is a quote from Ray Yao's website:</p>
<blockquote cite="www.amazon.com/author/ray-yao">
```

```
We sell both Paperbacks and Kindle books,
the searching keywords are:
Xxxxxx by Ray Yao
</blockquote>
// Output:
```

Here is a quote from Ray Yao's website:
We sell both Paperbacks and Kindle books, the searching keywords are:
Xxxxxx by Ray Yao

---

class syntax:

class="ClassName"

// Define a class that is used for Css.

e.g.

```
<style>
p.MyClass {color: green;}     // set Css by using MyClass
</style>
<p class="MyClass">Hello World!</p>     // define a class
// Output:   Hello World!
```

---

clearRect() syntax:

clearRect(x, y, width, height)

// Used to clear a specific rectangular area on the canvas, making it fully transparent by erasing any previously drawn content within the specified area.
// x: The x-coordinate of the rectangle's starting point (top-left corner).
// y: The y-coordinate of the rectangle's starting point.

e.g.

```
<canvas id="myCanvas" width="150" height="150"></canvas>
   <script>
      var ctx = document.getElementById('myCanvas').getContext('2d');
      ctx.fillStyle = "blue";
      ctx.fillRect(0, 0, 150, 150);   // Fill canvas with blue
      ctx.clearRect(30, 30, 90, 90);    // Clear a square in the center
   </script>
// Output:
```

---

clip() syntax:

context.clip();

// Creates a clipping path. Everything drawn after calling clip() will only appear inside the clipping region.

e.g.

```
<canvas id="myCanvas" width="130" height="90"></canvas>
<script>
 var canvas = document.getElementById('myCanvas');
 var context = canvas.getContext('2d');
 context.beginPath();   // Create a circular clipping path
 context.arc(50, 50, 30, 0, Math.PI * 2);
```

```
 context.clip();
 // Draw a green rectangle (only the part inside the circle will be visible)
 context.fillStyle = "green";
 context.fillRect(0, 0, 100, 100);
</script>
// Output:
```

---

closePath() syntax:

context.closePath();

// Close the current path by connecting the last point to the first point.

e.g.

```
<canvas id="cid" width="100" height="50" ></canvas>
<script>
var context = document.getElementById("cid").getContext("2d");
context.beginPath();
context.moveTo(0, 0);
context.lineTo(100, 50);
context.closePath();   // Close the line
context.stroke();
</script>
```

// Output:

---

color type syntax:

<input type="color">

// Used with <input> element to allow users to select a color by a color picker.

e.g.

```
<form>
 <label for="favcolor">Select your favorite color:</label>
 <input type="color" id="favcolor" name="favcolor">
</form>
```

// Output: Select your favorite color:

---

cols syntax:

<textarea rows="" cols="">

// Specify the width of a text area.

e.g.

```
<textarea rows="3" cols="40">
About the size of this textarea:
The row of this textarea is 3
The cols of this textarea is 20
</textarea>
```

// Output:

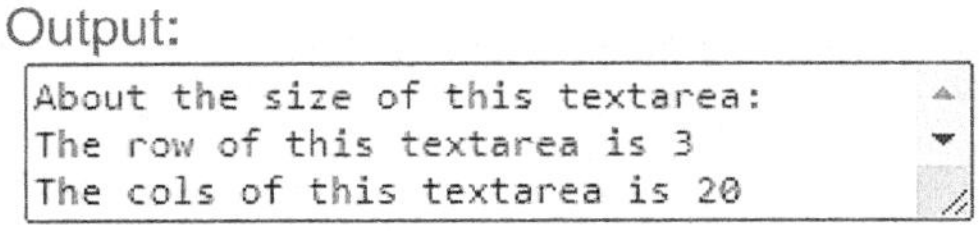

---

colspan syntax:

```
<td width="" rowspan="" colspan="">
// "width" sets the width of a cell
// "rowspan" sets the numbers of rows to span across.
// "colspan" sets the numbers of column to span across.
e.g.
<table border = "1" >
<tr><td width=300 colspan = 3>Cell 1</td></tr>
<tr><td>Cell 2</td><td>Cell 3</td><td>Cell 4</td></tr>
</table>
// Output:
```

Cell 1		
Cell 2	Cell 3	Cell 4

---

content syntax:

```
<meta name="" content="">
<meta http-equiv="" content="">
// Specify meta value of the name/content or http-equiv/content.
e.g.
<head>
<meta name="description" content="Html Cheat Sheet">
// provide a short description of the page
<meta http-equiv="content-language" content="en-us">
// set the language intended for the user
</head>
```

---

contenteditable syntax:

```
<p contenteditable="true/false">text</p>
// Specify a text as editable by setting contenteditable="true".
e.g.
<p contenteditable="true">This text is editable</p>
// Output:   This text is editable
```

---

context syntax:

```
var context = canvas.getContext('2d');
// `context` refers to the drawing context of the HTML <canvas> element. It is
used to render 2D shapes, images, text, and more on the canvas.
e.g.
<canvas id="myCanvas" width="130" height="90"></canvas>
<script>
  var canvas = document.getElementById('myCanvas');
  var context = canvas.getContext('2d');
  context.fillStyle = "green";    // Draw a simple green rectangle
  context.fillRect(10, 10, 50, 50);
</script>
// Output:
```

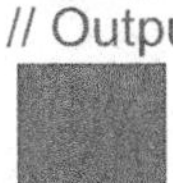

---

controls syntax:

```
<audio controls>
<source src="audio_file" type="audio/mpeg">
</audio>
```

// Embed an audio control to the current page

```
<video controls>
<source src="video_file" type="video/mp4">
</video>
```

// Embed a video control to the current page.

e.g. See <audio controls> syntax and <video controls> syntax.

---

controls syntax:

video_id.controls

// Enable, disable or check the video.

e.g.

```
<button onclick="fun1()" type="button">Enable Video</button>
<button onclick="fun2()" type="button">Disable Video</button>
<button onclick="fun3()" type="button">Check Video </button><br>
<video id="v" width="300" height="180">
<source src="myVideo.mp4" type="video/mp4">
</video>
<script>
function fun1() {  v.controls = true;  v.load(); }
function fun2() {  v.controls = false;   v.load(); }
function fun3() {  alert( "Is the video enabled? " + v.controls); }
</script>  // assume that we have enabled a video and check its status
```

// Output: [Enable Video] [Disable Video] [Check Video]

Is the video enabled? true

---

coords syntax:

```
<map>
<area shape="", coords="", href="", alt="">
</map>
```

// <map> defines an image map with clickable area.

// <area> defines a clickable area inside the image map, which can redirect to another specified page.

// "shape" specifies the shape of the area.

// "coords" specifies the coordinates of an area in an image map.

// "href" sets the url of the page. "alt" sets an alternate text.

e.g. please see the example of <map> syntax or <area> syntax.

---

createImageData() syntax:

let imageData = canvas.createImageData(width, height);

// Creates a new ImageData object with the specified width and height. This object stores pixel data for the canvas, where each pixel's color is represented by four values (red, green, blue, and alpha).

e.g.

```
<canvas id="myCanvas" width="160" height="160"></canvas>
```

```
<script>
 const canvas = document.getElementById('myCanvas');
 const ctx = canvas.getContext('2d');
 // Create a 60x60 ImageData object
 const imageData = ctx.createImageData(60, 60);
 // Set all pixels to blue (RGBA: 0, 0, 255, 255)
 for (let i = 0; i < imageData.data.length; i += 4) {
  imageData.data[i + 2] = 255;   // Blue
  imageData.data[i + 3] = 255;   // Alpha (fully opaque)
 }
 // Draw the blue square at (60, 60) on the canvas
 ctx.putImageData(imageData, 60, 60);
</script>
// Output:
```

---

createLinearGradient() syntax:

context.createLinearGradient(x1, y1, x2, y2)

// Create a linear gradient on canvas

x1	The x-coordinate of the gradient starting point
y1	The y-coordinate of the gradient starting point
x2	The x-coordinate of the gradient ending point
y2	The y-coordinate of the gradient ending point

e.g.

```
<canvas id="cid" width="200" height="100"></canvas>
<script>
var context = cid.getContext("2d");
var gradient = context.createLinearGradient(0, 0, 200, 100);
gradient.addColorStop(0, "green");   // set offset and color
gradient.addColorStop(1, "white");   // set offset and color
context.fillStyle = gradient;
context.fillRect(10, 5, 180, 90);
</script>
```

// Output: 

---

createPattern() syntax:

context.createPattern(image, direction)

// Create an image patter for canvas by the specific direction.

repeat	The pattern repeats both horizontally and vertically
repeat-x	The pattern repeats only horizontally
repeat-y	The pattern repeats only vertically
no-repeat	The pattern does not repeat.

e.g.

```
<img src="flower.jpg" id="imgid" width="50" height="50">
```

```
<canvas id="cid" width="300" height="85" style="border:1px solid"></canvas>
<button onclick="fun('repeat-x')">Repeat</button>
<script>
function fun(direction){
 var context = cid.getContext("2d");
 context.clearRect(0, 0, cid.width, cid.height);   // clear rectangle
 var patt = context.createPattern(imgid, direction);   // create pattern
 context.rect(0, 0, 300, 80);
 context.fillStyle = patt;
 context.fill();
}
</script>
// Output:
```

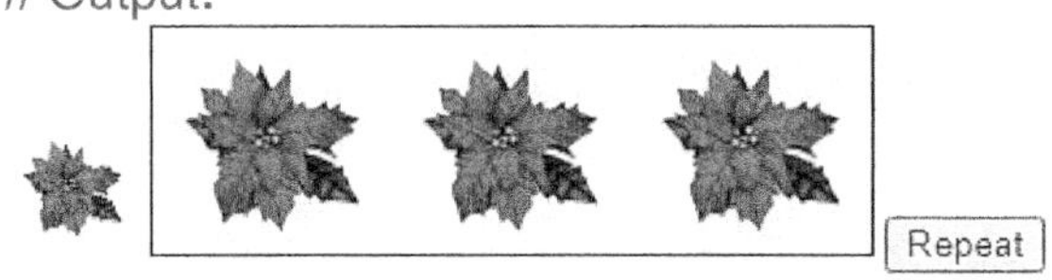

---

createRadialGradient() syntax:

context.createRadialGradient(x1, y2, r1, x2, y2, r2);

// Create a radial gradient on canvas

x1	The x-coordinate of the gradient start point
y1	The y-coordinate of the gradient start point
r1	The radius of the starting circle
x2	The x-coordinate of the gradient end point
y2	The y-coordinate of the gradient end point
r2	The radius of the ending circle

e.g.

```
<canvas id="cid" width="200" height="100"></canvas>
<script>
var context = cid.getContext("2d");
var gradient = context.createRadialGradient(100, 50, 20, 100, 50, 80);
gradient.addColorStop(0, "green");   // set offset and color
gradient.addColorStop(1, "white");   // set offset and color
context.fillStyle = gradient;
context.fillRect(10, 5, 180, 90);
</script>
```

// Output:

---

currentSrc syntax:

media_id.currentSrc

// Get the current url of an audio/video

e.g.

```
<button onclick="fun()" type="button">Get Media Url</button><br>
<video id="v" width="300" height="180" controls>
```

```
<source src="myVideo.mp4" type="video/mp4">
</video>
<script>
function fun() { alert(v.currentSrc);}
</script>
```

// Output: [Get Media Url] https://www.xxxxxxx.com/myVideo.mp4

---

currentTime syntax:

video_id.currentTime // get current time of a video playing
video_id.currentTime=value // set current time of a video playing

e.g.

```
<button onclick="fun1()" type="button">Get Current Time</button>
<button onclick="fun2()" type="button">Set Time to 2s</button><br>
<video id="v" width="300" height="180" controls>
<source src="myVideo.mp4" type="video/mp4">
</video>
<script>
function fun1() { alert(v.currentTime);}
function fun2() { v.currentTime=2;}   // set to 2 seconds
</script>
```

// Output:

[Get Current Time] [Set Time to 2s]

---

data syntax:

<object data = "" type = "" width = "" height = ""> </object>

// Embed all kinds of resources into the html document.
// "data" attribute specifies the resource url, it can be an image, a file...
// "type" attribute specifies the MIME type of the resource.

e.g.(1)

```
<object data="flower.jpg" type="image/jpeg" width="100" height="100">
</object>
```

// Output:

e.g. (2)

```
<object data="myDoc.html" type="text/html" width="300" height="200">
</object>
```

// Output: *Hello, I am an html file; I am embedded in the current HTML document. You are able to see me now!*

---

data-* syntax:

data-id="value"
// Attach a hidden data to an element. The data is invisible to user.
e.g.
<ol>
<li **data-id**="001" **data-price**="$1.99">Apples</li>
<li **data-id**="002" **data-price**="$2.99">Banana</li>
<li **data-id**="003" **data-price**="$3.99">Cherry</li>
</ol>
// Output:

1. Apples
2. Banana
3. Cherry

---

date type syntax:

<input type="date">
// Used with <input> element to allow users to select a date from a date picker.
e.g.
<form>
<label for="birthday">Select your birthday:</label>
<input **type="date"** id="birthday" name="birthday">
</form>
// Output: Select your birthday: [yyyy-mm-dd]

---

datetime-local type syntax:

<input type="datetime-local">
// Used to exist with the <input> element to capture both date and time.
e.g.
<form>
<label for="appointment">Schedule an appointment:</label>
<input **type="datetime-local"** id="meeting" name="meeting">
</form>
// Output: Schedule an appointment: [yyyy-mm-dd]

---

datetime using syntax:

<time datetime=""> text </time> // define a datetime
<ins datetime=""> text </ins> // attach a hidden datetime
<del datetime=""> text </del> // attach a hidden datetime
e.g.
<time **datetime="2023-01-01 00:00"**>New Year's Day</time>
<ins **datetime="2023-01-01 00:00"**> The inserted text </ins>
<del **datetime="2023-01-01 00:00"**> The deleted text </del>
// Output: New Year's Day Office Hours: 09:00 -- 17:00
The inserted text ~~The deleted text~~

---

default syntax:

<track src="" kind="" srclang="" label="" default>
// Define subtitle, caption, description for <audio> or <video> element.
// "src" specifies a track file. "kind" sets the subtitle, caption…

// "kind" specifies the kind of text track.
// "label" sets the title of the text track.
// "default" sets the track enabled unless user sets other preferences.
e.g. See the example <track> syntax

----

defaultPlaybackRate syntax:

media_id.defaultPlaybackRate // get speed of media playing
media_id.defaultPlaybackRate=value // set speed of media playing
e.g.

```
<button onclick="fun1()" type="button">Check Default  Speed</button>
<button onclick="fun2()" type="button">Set Default Speed</button><br>
<video id="vid" width="300" height="180" controls>
  <source src="myVideo.mp4" type="video/mp4">
</video>
<script>
function fun1() { alert("Default speed is: " + vid.defaultPlaybackRate);}
function fun2() { vid.defaultPlaybackRate=0.6;  vid.load(); }
</script>   // assume that we set default playing speed to 0.6
```

// Output: [Get Default Speed] [Set Default Speed] Default speed is: 0.6

----

defer syntax:

<script src="external.js" defer></script>
// Specify that an external JS file will run after the page has loaded.
e.g.

```
<script src="helloworld.js" defer></script>
```

// Given the contents of "helloworld.js" is: alert("Hello World!");
// Output: Hello World!

----

dir syntax:

<p dir="ltr"> text </p> // text direction from left to right
<p dir="rtl"> text </p> // text direction from right to left
// Set the direction of the text
e.g.

```
<p dir="rtl">The direction of this text is from right to left!</p>
```

// Output:

!The direction of this text is from right to left

----

dirname syntax:

<input type="text" name="xxx" dirname="xxx.dir">
<textarea name="xxx" dirname="xxx.dir">
// Specify to submit the text direction together with the input value
// Note: the extension name of the "dirname" is ".dir".
e.g.

```
<form action="myFile.php">   // php file processes the inputted data
Name:<input type="text" name="n" dirname="n.dir">
<input type="submit" value="Submit">
</form>
```

// Output:

Name: [ ] [Submit]

// How to process the inputted data? Please see PHP Cheat Sheet

---

disabled syntax:

```
<element type=" " disabled>
```

// Set an element disabled

e.g.

```
<button type="button" disabled>Click Me!</button>
```

// Output:

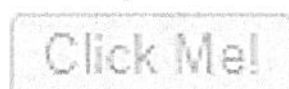

---

download syntax:

```
<a href="file" download></a>
```

// Specify that a file can be downloaded when being clicked.

e.g.

```
<p>Click on the flower to download the image:<p>
<a href="flower.jpg" download>
<img src="flower.jpg" alt="flower">
</a>
```

// Output: Click on the flower to download the image:

---

draggable syntax:

```
draggable="true/false"
```

// Specify an element is draggable if true, is not draggable if false.
// "draggable property" needs to work with JavaScript together.
// Learn more "draggable property"? Read related JavaScript book.

e.g.

```
<script> ......JavaScript event code ...... </script>
<p draggable="true">This is a draggable text.</p>
```

// Output: This is a draggable text.

---

drawImage() syntax:

```
context.drawImage(image, x, y, width, height)
```

// Draw an image, audio, or video onto the canvas.
// "x" is the x coordinate where the image/media is drawn to the canvas
// "y" is the y coordinate where the image/media is drawn to the canvas

e.g.

```
<img id="imgid" src="flower.jpg" alt="flower" width="100" height="100">
<canvas id="cid" width="100" height="100" style="border:1px solid"></canvas>
<script>
function fun(){
var context = cid.getContext("2d");
context.drawImage(imgid,0,0);      // draw an image to the canvas
}
</script>
<br><button onclick="fun()">Click me to draw image to canvas</button>
```

// Output:

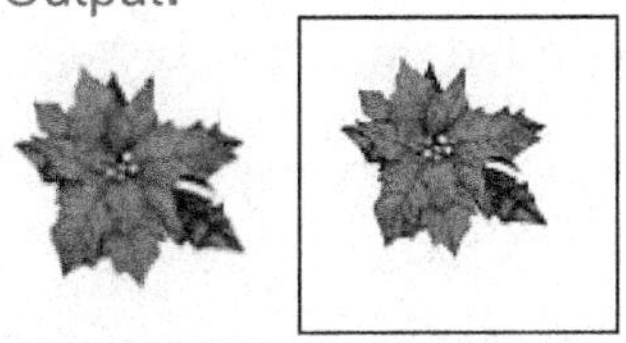

Click me to draw image to canvas

---

duration syntax:

video_id.duration

// Get the video length

e.g.

```
<button onclick="fun()" type="button">Video Duration</button><br>
<video id="v" width="300" height="180" controls>
  <source src="myVideo.mp4" type="video/mp4">
</video>
<script>
function fun(){ alert( "The video length is: " + v.duration); }
</script>    // Given the length of the video is 59.002
```

// Output: Video Duration The video length is: 59.992

---

email type syntax:

<input type="email" name="user-email">

// The email type in HTML is used for input fields where the user is expected to enter an email address. It provides basic validation to ensure the entered text matches the pattern of a valid email address.

e.g.

```
<p>Enter your email:</p>
   <form>
      <input type="email" id="email" name="email">
      <input type="submit" value="Submit">
</form>
```

// Output: Enter your email:

Submit

---

enctype syntax:

<form action="" method="post" enctype="multipart/form-data">

// Specify how to encode the form data when being submitted to server.

e.g.

```
<form action="" method="post" enctype="multipart/form-data">
Name:<input type="text" id="name">
<input type="submit" value="Submit">
</form>
```

// Output: Name: Submit

---

ended syntax:

video_id.ended

// Return true if the video complete playing, return false if not.

e.g.
```
<button onclick="fun()" type="button">Check Video Ended</button><br>
<video id="v" width="300" height="180" controls>
  <source src="myVideo.mp4" type="video/mp4">
</video>
<script>
function fun(){ alert( "Video ended? " + v.ended); }
</script>   // assume that the video is playing currently
// Output:   Check Video Ended    Video ended?  false
```

---

file type syntax:

<input type="file">

// Used with <input> element to allow users to upload files from their device.

e.g.
```
<form>
  <label for="upload">Select a file to upload:</label>
  <input type="file" id="upload" name="upload">
</form>
// Output:   Select a file to upload:   Choose File   No file chosen
```

---

fill() syntax:

context.fill();

// Fill the current or specified path with the current fillStyle (color, gradient, or pattern). It fills all the enclosed shapes defined by the current path.

e.g.
```
<canvas id="myCanvas" width="150" height="150" style="border:1px solid black;"></canvas>
  <script>
    // Get the canvas element and its context
    var canvas = document.getElementById('myCanvas');
    var ctx = canvas.getContext('2d');
    ctx.beginPath();   // Begin the path to draw a triangle
    ctx.moveTo(0, 0);   // Start at this point
    ctx.lineTo(150, 50);   // Draw line to this point
    ctx.lineTo(100, 150);   // Draw line to this point
    ctx.closePath();   // Close the path
    ctx.fillStyle = "green";   // Set the fill color
    ctx.fill();   // Fill the triangle
  </script>
// Output:
```

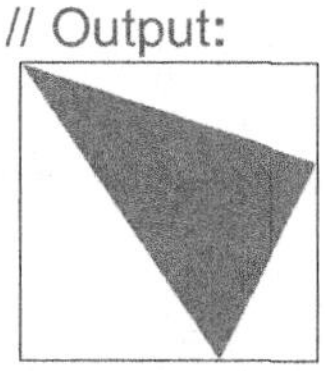

---

fillRect() syntax:

context.fillRect(x, y, width, height)

// Draw a rectangle and fill with specific color. (fill black by default).
// "x" is the x-coordinate of the upper-left corner of the rectangle.
// "y" is the y-coordinate of the upper-left corner of the rectangle.

e.g.

```
<canvas id="cid" width="100" height="50"></canvas>
<script>
var context = cid.getContext("2d");     // return a canvas context
context.fillStyle = "green";        // fill the rectangle with green
context.fillRect(0, 0, 100, 50);     // draw a rectangle
</script>
// Output:
```

---

fillStyle syntax:

context.fillStyle="color/gradient/pattern"

// fill the specified color, gradient, or pattern to the canvas context.

e.g.

```
<canvas id="cid" width="100" height="50"></canvas>
<script>
var context = cid.getContext("2d");  // return a canvas context
context.fillStyle = "green";       // fill the rectangle with green
context.fillRect(0,0,100,50);    // draw a rectangle
</script>
// Output:
```

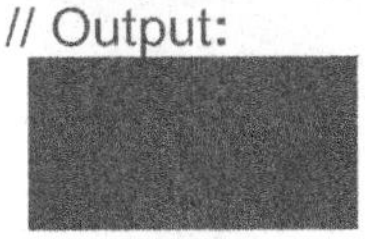

---

fillText() syntax:

context.fillText("text", x, y);

// Draw text with filled on the canvas. The text is black by default.
// "x" is the x- coordinate where to begin drawing the text
// "y" is the y- coordinate where to begin drawing the text

```
<canvas id="cid" width="100" height="50" ></canvas>
<script>
var context = cid.getContext("2d");
context.font = "15px Arial black";     // set a font
context.fillText("Hello World", 5, 25);     // draw text
</script>
// Output:    Hello World
```

---

font attribute syntax:

context.font="value"

// Set of get a font property for the text on canvas

```
<canvas id="cid" width="100" height="50" ></canvas>
<script>
var context = cid.getContext("2d");
context.font = "15px Arial black";      // set a font
context.fillText("Hello World", 5, 25);
</script>
// Output:    Hello World
```

---

font style syntax:

{ property: value }

// Set the font style

property	Value
font-family	arial, times new roman, courier new, georgia, verdana
font-size	9px, 10px……large
font-style	normal, italic, oblique
font-weight	normal, bold, number
font-variant	normal, small-caps
color	red, yellow, green, blue……

e.g.

<style type = "text/css">

#f{ **font-family: Times New Roman; font-size: 28px; font-style: italic; font-weight: bold; font-variant: normal; color: green** }

</style>

<div id = "f">This is a text content using a different style.</div>

// Output:

This is a text content using a different style.

---

for syntax:

<label for="element_id"></label>

// Specify which element the label is bound to.

e.g.

<form action="myFile.php">

<label **for="name"**>Name:</label>

<input type="text" id="**name**">

<input type="submit" value="Submit">

</form>

// Output: Name: [ ] [Submit]

---

for syntax:

<output id="" for="id1 id2"></output>

// Represent which elements the computed output comes from.

e.g.

<form oninput="sum.value=parseInt(x.value)+parseInt(y.value);">

<input type="number" id="x" value=""/>

\+

<input type="number" id="y" value=""/>

=

Result: **<output id="sum" for="x y"></output>**

</form> // the sum comes from x and y elements

// Output:

10

\+

20

=

Result: 30

---

form syntax:

```
form = "form_id"
```

// Indicate the element belongs to which form.

e.g

```
<form action="myFile.php" id="myForm">
Name:<input type="text" id="name">
<input type="submit" value="Submit">
</form>
*Note:<input type="text" id="note" form="myForm">
```

// Output:

Name: [ ] [Submit]

*Note: [ ]

---

formaction syntax:

```
<input type="submit" formaction="myFile.php" value="Submit">
```

// Specify which page to send the form data to when a form is submitted

e.g.

```
<form action="file1.php">   // send data to file1.php for processing
Name:<input type="text" id="n">
<input type="submit" value="Submit1"><br>
Submit to another page:
<input type="submit" formaction="file2.php" value="Submit2">
</form>     // send data to file2.php for processing
```

// Output:

Name: [ ] [Submit1]

Submit to another page: [Submit2]

---

getContext syntax:

```
var context = canvas_id.getContext('2d');
```

// Get a rendering context which is used to draw, fill and modify canvas.

e.g.

```
<canvas id="cid" width="100" height="50"></canvas>
<script>
var context = cid.getContext("2d");   // return a canvas context
context.fillStyle = "green";       // fill the rectangle with green
context.fillRect(0,0,100,50);      // draw a rectangle
</script>
```

// Output:

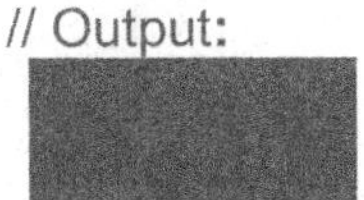

---

getImageData() syntax:

let imageData = ctx.getImageData(x, y, width, height);

// Returns an ImageData object that contains the pixel data for a specific rectangular area of the canvas. ImageData stores pixel data for the canvas, where pixel's color is represented by four values (red, green, blue, and alpha).
// x, y: The coordinates of the top-left corner of the rectangle from which the pixel data is to be extracted.

e.g.

```
<canvas id="myCanvas" width="100" height="100"></canvas>
<script>
  const canvas = document.getElementById('myCanvas');
  const ctx = canvas.getContext('2d');
  ctx.fillStyle = "green";   // Create a green rectangle
  ctx.fillRect(0, 0, 100, 100);
  // Get image data for the entire canvas (100x100 pixels)
  let imageData = ctx.getImageData(0, 0, 100, 100);
  // Log pixel data for the first pixel (top-left corner)
  console.log(imageData.data[0], imageData.data[1], imageData.data[2],
imageData.data[3]);    // [255, 0, 0, 255] -> green color with full opacity
</script>
// Output:
```

---

globalAlpha syntax:

context.globalAlpha = value;

// `globalAlpha` is a property of the Canvas 2D API that sets the transparency (alpha) level of all drawing operations on the canvas. The value of globalAlpha is a number between 0.0 (fully transparent) and 1.0 (fully opaque).

e.g.

```
<canvas id="myCanvas" width="120" height="90"></canvas>
<script>
  var ctx = document.getElementById('myCanvas').getContext('2d');
  ctx.fillStyle = "red";   // Fully opaque red rectangle
  ctx.fillRect(10, 10, 50, 50);
  ctx.globalAlpha = 0.3;   // Semi-transparent blue rectangle
  ctx.fillStyle = "blue";
  ctx.fillRect(30, 30, 50, 50);
</script>
// Output:
```

---

globalCompositieOperation syntax:

context.globalCompositeOperation = type;

// `globalCompositeOperation` is a property of the Canvas 2D API that determines how new shapes are drawn over existing content on the canvas. It defines how two shapes overlap, blending or masking one over the other. The `type` specifies the compositing or blending operation to use when drawing new content over existing content.

e.g.

```
<canvas id="myCanvas" width="120" height="90"></canvas>
<script>
 var ctx = document.getElementById('myCanvas').getContext('2d');
 ctx.fillStyle = "green";   // Draw a green rectangle
 ctx.fillRect(10, 10, 50, 50);
 // Set globalCompositeOperation to 'destination-over'
 ctx.globalCompositeOperation = "destination-over";
 // Draw a red rectangle (it will appear behind the green one)
 ctx.fillStyle = "red";
 ctx.fillRect(30, 30, 50, 50);
</script>
```

// Output:

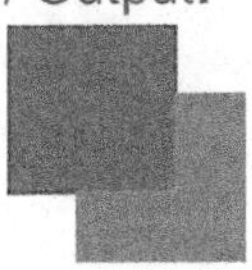

---

header syntax:

```
headers="element_id"
```

// Specify the current element is related to a <th> element by id

e.g.

```
<table>
<tr><th id="name">Name</th><th id="age">Age</th></tr>
<tr><td headers="name">Andy</td><td headers="age">18</td></tr>
</table>
```

// Output:

Name	Age
Andy	18

---

height syntax:

```
<img src=""  width=""  height=""  alt=""></img>
<iframe src="" width="" height=""></iframe>
<canvas id="" width="" height=""></canvas>
<object data="" width="" height=""></object>
<embed src="" width="" height=""></embed>
<video width="" height="" controls></video>
<input type="image" src="" width="" height="">
```

// Specify the height of the element.

e.g. Please see the examples of above elements.

---

hidden syntax:

```
<p hidden> text </p>
```

// Set a hidden text

e.g.

```
<p>You cannot see the paragraph below!</p>
```

<p **hidden**>This text is hidden.</p>
// Output: You cannot see the paragraph below!

----

hidden type syntax:

<input type="hidden" name="field-name" value="field-value">
// Used with the <input> element to store data that is not visible to the user but is sent when the form is submitted.
e.g.
<form>
<input type="hidden" name="myID" value="100">
<button **type="submit"**>Submit</button>
</form>
// Output: Submit

----

high syntax:

<meter id="" min="" max="" low="" high="" value=""></meter>
// The "high" sets the range where the gauge's value is considered to be a high value.
// The "low" sets the range where the gauge's value is considered to be a low value.
// The "max" sets the upper bound of the gauge.
// The "min" sets the lower bound of the gauge.
// The "value" sets the current value of the gauge.
e.g.
<body>
<label for="a">Andy's Score:</label>
<meter id="a" min="0" max="100" low="35" **high="95"** value="60"></meter>
<label for="b">Betty's Score:</label>
<meter id="b" min="0" max="100" low="35" **high="95"** value="85"></meter>
</body>
// Output:
Andy's Score:
Betty's Score:

----

href syntax:

<a href="url"> text </a>
// Specify the link's to a web site
<link rel="stylesheet" type="text/css" href="external.css">
// Link to an external stylesheet
e.g.
<a **href**="https://www.amazon.com">Visit Amazon</a>
// Output: Visit Amazon

----

hreflang syntax:

<a href="url" hreflang="language"> text </a>
// Specify a language of the web site in the link
<link href="myFile" rel="" rev="" hreflang="en">
// Specify a language of the file in the link
e.g.
<a href="https://www.amazon.com" **hreflang="en"**>Visit Amazon</a>
// Output: Visit Amazon

----

http-equiv syntax:

<meta http-equiv="value" content="">
// Provide header information or content attribute's value
e.g.
<head>
<meta **http-equiv**="refresh" content="20">
// Refresh the page ever 20
<meta **http-equiv**="content-security-policy" content="default-src https:">
// Specify a content security policy for the resource.
<meta **http-equiv**="content-type" content="text/html; charset=US-ASCII">
// Specify the character set encoding for the document.
<meta **http-equiv**="default-style" content="default stylesheet">
// Specify the default style sheet to use
</head>

----

hyperlink style syntax:

a:link{attribute: value;}
a:hover{attribute: value;}
a:active{ attribute: value;}
a:visited{ attribute: value;}
// **Link:** the link has never been clicked before.
// **Hover:** the cursor is placed over the hyperlink.
// **Active:** the link is being clicked by a user.
// **Visited:** the link has been clicked by the user previously.
e.g.
<style type = "text/css">
a:link {color: green;}
a:visited {color: blue;}
a:hover {color: red;}
a:active {color: purple;}
</style>
<a href = "https://www.amazon.com"> Welcome to Amazon </a>
// Output: Welcome to Amazon (after click) Welcome to Amazon

----

id syntax:

<element id = "">
// Specify a unique identity for an HTML element
e.g.
<style type = "text/css">
#myID{font-family: arial black;color: blue;}
</style>
Greeting: <span **id = "myID"**> Hello World!</span>
// Output: Greeting: **Hello World!**

----

image type syntax:

<input type="image" src="image-url" alt="Submit">
// Used with <input> element to create a clickable image that submits a form when clicked. It functions like a submit button but is displayed as an image.
e.g.
<form action="myfile.php">

```
  <label for="flower">What is this flower?</label><br>
  <input type="image" src="flower.jpg" alt="Submit" width="100" height="80">
</form>
// Output:   What is this flower?
```

---

ismap syntax:

```
<img src="" ismap>
// Specify that the image is used as a server-side image map.
// When the image is clicked, mouse coordinates will be send to server.
e.g.
<a href="/example/action.html">
<img src="flower.jpg" ismap><br>
When the image is clicked, the server will return the mouse coordinates.
</a>
// Output:
```

When the image is clicked, the server will return the mouse coordinates.
coordinate = 89, 168

---

isPointInPath() syntax:

```
context.isPointInPath(x, y);
// Checks whether a given point (x, y) is inside the current path. It returns true
if the point is inside the path and false otherwise.
// x: The x-coordinate of the point to test.
// y: The y-coordinate of the point to test.
e.g.
<canvas id="myCanvas" width="130" height="90"></canvas>
<script>
  var canvas = document.getElementById('myCanvas');
  var context = canvas.getContext('2d');
  context.beginPath();   // Create a rectangular path
  context.rect(20, 20, 100, 50);
  // Check if point (28, 28) is inside the rectangle
  var isInside = context.isPointInPath(28, 28);
  document.write("Is point (28, 28) inside the path? " + isInside);
</script>
// Output:    Is point (28, 28) inside the path? true
```

---

kind syntax:

```
<track src="" kind="" srclang="" label="" default>
// Define subtitle, caption, description for <audio> or <video> element.
// "src" specifies a track file. "kind" sets the subtitle, caption…
// "kind" specifies the kind of text track.
```

// "label" sets the title of the text track.
// "default" sets the track enabled unless user sets other preferences.
e.g. See the example <track> syntax

---

lang syntax:

lang="xx"
// specify the language of the element's text, such as en, de, es…
e.g.

```
<p lang="fr">Bonjour le monde!</p>
```

// Output: Bonjour le monde!

---

lineTo() syntax:

context.lineTo(x, y);
// Specify the ending point of the line in the canvas.
// "x" is the x-coordinate of the line's ending point.
// "y" is the y-coordinate of the line's ending point.
e.g.

```
<canvas id="cid" width="100" height="50" ></canvas>
<script>
var context = cid.getContext("2d");
context.moveTo(0, 0);
context.lineTo(100, 50);
context.stroke();
</script>
```

// Output: 

---

lineWidth syntax:

context.lineWidth = width;
// Set the width of lines and outlines of shapes drawn on the canvas.
e.g.

```
<canvas id="myCanvas" width="160" height="160" style="border:1px solid black;"></canvas>
  <script>
    var ctx = document.getElementById('myCanvas').getContext('2d');
    ctx.lineWidth = 10;   // Set the line width
    ctx.beginPath();   // Draw a line with the specified line width
    ctx.moveTo(20, 20);
    ctx.lineTo(140, 140);
    ctx.stroke();
  </script>
```

// Output:

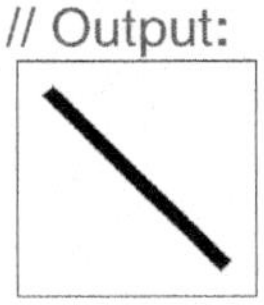

---

list syntax:

<input list="element_id" name="" id="">
// Define an id value for <datalist> element.

```
// <datalist> defines an optional value for an input control.
e.g.
<form action="" method="get">
  Select your favorite fruit:
  <input list="fruits" name="fr" id="fr">
  <datalist id="fruits">
    <option value="Apple">
    <option value="Banana">
    <option value="Cherry">
  </datalist>
  <input type="submit">
</form>
// Output:
```

Select your favorite fruit: [ ] [Submit]

---

load() syntax:

video_id.load()

```
// Load a new video according to its id
e.g.
<button onclick="fun()" type="button">Change Video</button><br>
<video id="vid" width="300" height="180" controls autoplay>
  <source  src="video1.mp4" type="video/mp4">
  <source  src="video2.mp4" type="video/mp4">
</video>
<script>
function fun() { vid.src = "video2.mp4"; vid.load(); }
</script>
// Output:
```

[Change Video]

video1

video2

---

loop syntax:

<audio controls loop>...</audio>
<video controls loop>...</video>

// Set that the audio/video starts over again when it is completed.
e.g. please see the example of <audio> syntax or <video> syntax.

---

loop syntax:

video_id.loop = true/false // enable or disable the video loop
video_id.loop // return true if video can loop, return false if not

```
e.g.
<button onclick="fun1()" type="button">Enable Loop</button>
<button onclick="fun2()" type="button">Disable Loop</button>
<button onclick="fun3()" type="button">Check Loop</button><br>
```

```
<video id="v" width="300" height="180" controls>
  <source src="myVideo.mp4" type="video/mp4">
</video>
<script>
function fun1(){ v.loop = true; v.load(); }
function fun2(){ v.loop = false; v.load(); }
function fun3(){ alert( "The video loop? " + v.loop); }
</script>    // assume that the loop has been enabled currently.
// Output:   [Enable Loop] [Disable Loop] [Check Loop]    The video loop? true
```

---

low syntax:

```
<meter id="" min="" max="" low="" high="" value=""></meter>
// The "high" sets the range where the gauge's value is considered to be a high value.
// The "low" sets the range where the gauge's value is considered to be a low value.
// The "max" sets the upper bound of the gauge.
// The "min" sets the lower bound of the gauge.
// The "value" sets the current value of the gauge.
e.g.
<body>
<label for="a">Andy's Score:</label>
<meter id="a" min="0" max="100" low="35" high="95" value="60"></meter>
<label for="b">Betty's Score:</label>
<meter id="b" min="0" max="100" low="35" high="95" value="85"></meter>
</body>
// Output:
```

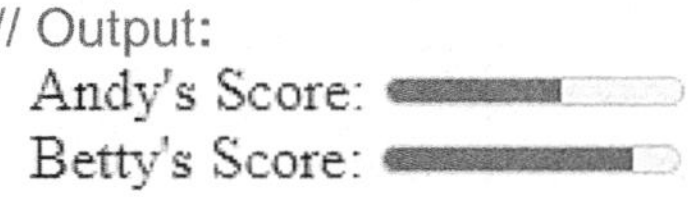

---

margin syntax:

```
margin: value
// The margin is the area around the border edges.
// The margin width can be specified with a margin attribute.
e.g.
<style type = "text/css">
#b1{border-style: solid; border-width: 5px; margin: 30px }
#b2{border-style: dotted; border-width: 5px; margin: 0px }
</style>
<p id = "b1">This margin is 30px.</p>
<p id = "b2">This margin is 0px.</p>
// Output:
```

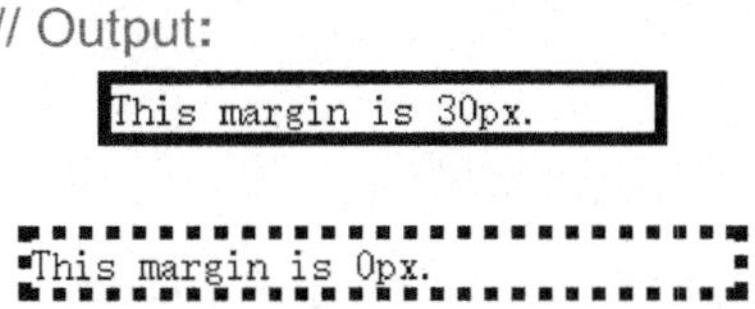

---

max syntax:

```
<input type="number" min="" max="">
<meter min="" max="" value=""></meter>
<progress max="" value=""></progress>
```

// Specify the maximum value of the element
e.g.

```
<input type="number" name="quantity" min="0" max="10">
<input type="submit">
```

// Output 10 Submit

---

maxlength syntax:

```
<input type="text" id="" maxlength="">
<textarea id="" rows="" cols="" maxlength="">
```

// Specify the maximum number of characters that can be entered.
e.g.

```
Name: <input type="text" id="n" maxlength="12">
<input type="submit" value="Submit">
```

// Output: Name: Submit

---

measureText() syntax:

var textMetrics = context.measureText(text);

// Used to obtain the width of a specified text string, and returns a TextMetrics object containing the width of the text.
e.g.

```
<canvas id="myCanvas" width="200" height="80" style="border:1px solid black;"></canvas>
  <script>
    var canvas = document.getElementById('myCanvas');
    var ctx = canvas.getContext('2d');
    ctx.font = "20px Arial";    // Set font style
    var text = "Ray Yao's Books!";
    var textMetrics = ctx.measureText(text);    // Measure the text
    ctx.fillText(text, 10, 50);    // Draw the text
    ctx.beginPath();    // Draw a line showing the width of the text
    ctx.moveTo(10, 60);
    ctx.lineTo(10 + textMetrics.width, 60);
    ctx.strokeStyle = "red";
    ctx.stroke();
  </script>
```

// Output:

---

media syntax:

<element media="device and (value)"/>

// Specify the optimal media or device for a resource or a link.
e.g.

```
<a href="/tutorial/print.html" media="print and (resolution:290dpi)"> Click
device link for print.</a>
```

// Output: Click device link for print.

---

method syntax:

<form action="myFile.php" method="get/post">

```
// Specify the http method to send data to server.
// "get" method sends data to the server openly, small quantity.
// "post" method sends data to the server secretly, more quantity.
// To learn more how to process data, Please see PHP Cheat Sheet.
e.g.
<form action="myFile.php" method="post">
name: <input type="text" name="n">
<input type="submit">
</form>
// Output:
```

name: [   ] [Submit]

---

min syntax:

```
<input type="number" min="" max="">
<meter min="" max="" value=""></meter>
// Specify the minimum value of the element
e.g.
<input type="number" name="quantity" min="0" max="10">
<input type="submit">
```

// Output [0] [Submit]

---

month type syntax:

```
<input type="month">
// Used with the <input> element to allow users to select a specific month and
year without choosing a day.
e.g.
<form>
  <label for="promotion-month">Select promotion month:</label>
  <input type="month" id="promotion-month" name="promotion-month">
</form>
```

// Output: Select promotion month: [--------- ----]

---

moveTo() syntax:

```
context.moveTo(x, y);
// Specify the starting point of the line in the canvas.
// "x" is the x-coordinate of the line's starting point.
// "y" is the y-coordinate of the line's starting point.
e.g.
<canvas id="cid" width="100" height="50" ></canvas>
<script>
var context = cid.getContext("2d");
context.moveTo(0, 0);
context.lineTo(100, 50);
context.stroke();
</script>
```

// Output: 

---

multiple syntax:

```
<input type="" name="" multiple>
<select multiple>…</select>
// Specify that user can input multiple values or select multiple files.
e.g.
<form action="myFile.php">
Select more than one files:
<input type="file" name="f" multiple><br>
<input type="submit">
</form>
// Output:
```

Select more than one files: [Choose Files] No file chosen
[Submit]

---

muted syntax:

```
<video controls muted>
// Specify that the video is muted, the video can play without sound.
e.g.
<video controls muted>
<source src="/media/movie.mp4" type="video/mp4">
</video>
// Output:
```

---

muted syntax:

```
video_id.muted = true/false    // enable or disable the video muted
video_id.muted     // return true if video is muted, return false if not
e.g.
<button onclick="fun1()" type="button">Enable Muted</button>
<button onclick="fun2()" type="button">Disable Muted</button>
<button onclick="fun3()" type="button">Check Muted</button><br>
<video id="v" width="300" height="180" controls>
  <source src="myVideo.mp4" type="video/mp4">
</video>
<script>
function fun1(){ v.muted = true; }
function fun2(){ v.muted = false; }
function fun3(){ alert( "The video muted? " + v.muted); }
</script>    // assume that the muted has been enabled currently.
// Output:
```

[Enable Muted] [Disable Muted] [Check Muted]   The video muted? true

---

name syntax:

```
<element type="" name="">
<form action="" method="" name=""></form>
// Define a name of the element
e.g.
```

```
<form action="myFile.php">  // php file processes the inputted data
Please enter your email:<br>
<input type="email" name="myEmail" >  <input type="submit">
</form>
// Output:   Please enter your email:
             [                    ] [Submit]
```

---

networkState syntax:

media_id.networkState

// Get a network state number of a media. The network state number is:

"0"	media has not yet been initialized.
"1"	media is active with a resource, but not by network
"2"	media is downloading resource by network
"3"	media resource is not found

e.g.

```
<button onclick="fun()" type="button">Get Network State</button><br>
<video id="v" width="300" height="180" controls>
<source src="myVideo.mp4" type="video/mp4">
</video>
<script>
function fun() { alert("The current network state is " + v.networkState);}
</script>
// Output:   [Get Network State]    The current network state is  1
```

---

novalidate syntax:

<form action="" method="" novalidate></form>

// Specify that the form should not be validated when submitted

e.g.

```
<form action="myFile.php" novalidate>
Please enter your email:<br>
<input type="email" name="myEmail" >  <input type="submit">
</form>
// Output:   Please enter your email:
             [                    ] [Submit]
```

---

number type syntax:

<input type="number" id="…" name="…" min="…" max="…" step="…">

// This is an attribute used with the <input> element to allow users to enter numeric values.

// The min attribute sets the minimum allowed value.

// The max attribute sets the maximum allowed value.

// The step attribute specifies the increments.

e.g.

```
<form>
<label for="quantity">Enter a number:</label>
<input type="number" id="quantity" name="quantity" min="1" max="10">
</form>
```

// Output: Enter a number: [ ]

---

onabort syntax:

<element onabort="function()">

// Run function() when the loading of a media is aborted.

e.g.

```
<img src="myPhoto.jpg" onabort="fun()">
<script>    // run a JavaScript function
function fun(){ alert("Loading is aborted!"); }
</script>
```

// Output: Loading is aborted!

---

onafterprint syntax:

<body onafterprint="function()">

// Run function() when a page has started printing.

e.g.

```
<body onafterprint="fun()">
<p> Press Ctrl+P to print:</p>
<script>    // run a JavaScript function
function fun(){ alert("The page has started printing!"); }
</script>
</body>
```

// Output: Press Ctrl+P to print: The page has started printing!

---

onbeforeprint syntax:

<body onbeforeprint="function()">

// Run function() when a page is going to be printed.

e.g.

```
<body onbeforeprint="fun()">
<p> Press Ctrl+P to print:</p>
<script>    // run a JavaScript function
function fun(){ alert("The page is going to be printed!"); }
</script>
</body>
```

// Output: Press Ctrl+P to print: The page is going to be printed!

---

onbeforeunload syntax:

<body onbeforeunload="return jsFunction()">

// Display a default message when the page is going to unload.

e.g.

```
<body onbeforeunload="return fun()">
<a href="https://www.amazon.com">Visit Amazon</a>
<script>    // show a default message when going to another site.
function fun(){
return "";
}
</script>
</body>
```

// Output: Visit Amazon

```
Leave site?
Changes you made may not be saved.
```

---

onblur syntax:

```
<element type="" id="" onblur="function()">
// Run function() when an element loses focus.
e.g.
Name:<input type="text" id="n" onblur="fun()">
<script>  // run a JavaScript function when outside text field is clicked
function fun(){alert("The text field loses focus!");}
</script>
// Output:   Name:

            The text field loses focus!
```

---

oncanplay syntax:

```
<audio oncanplay="function()">
<video oncanplay="function()">
// Run function() when a media can start to play.
e.g.
<video id="myVideo" width="300" height="200" controls oncanplay="fun()">
<source src="myVideo.mp4" type="video/mp4">
</video>
<script>
function fun() {    // run a JavaScript function
alert("The video can start to play now!");
}
</script>
// Output:   The video can start to play now!
```

---

oncanplaythrough syntax:

```
<audio oncanplaythrough="function()">
<video oncanplaythrough="function()">
// Run function() when the browser estimates it can completely play the
specified audio/video without having to stop for buffering.
e.g.
<video id="myVideo" width="300" height="200" controls
oncanplaythrough="fun()">
<source src="myVideo.mp4" type="video/mp4">
</video>
<script>
function fun() {    // run a JavaScript function
alert("The video can completely play without any stop for buffering!");
}
```

</script>
// Output: The video can completely play without any stop for buffering!

----

onchange syntax:

<select onchange="function()"> </select>
// Run function() when the value of the element is changed.
e.g.
<select **onchange="fun()"**>
<option value="a">Apple
<option value="b">Banana
<option value="c">Cherry
</select>
<script> // run JavaScript function when select one of the options
function fun(){ alert("The value of the element is changed!"); }
</script>

// Output: Banana ▾

The value of the element is changed!

----

onclick syntax:

<element onclick="function()">
// Run function() when the element is clicked.
e.g.
<button **onclick="fun()"**>Click Me</button>
<script> // run a JavaScript function
function fun(){ alert("The button is clicked!"); }
</script>

// Output: Click Me

The button is clicked!

----

oncontextmenu syntax:

<element oncontextmenu="function()">
// Run function() when the specific element is right-clicked.
// Then the context menu will pop up.
e.g.
<textarea **oncontextmenu="fun()"**>
Please right click here!
</textarea>
<script> // run a JavaScript function
function fun(){ alert("The context menu is about to show!"); }
</script>

// Output: Please right click here!

The context menu is about to show!

---

oncopy syntax:

<element type="" oncopy="function()">

// Run function() when the content of the element is copied.

e.g.

```
<input type="text" oncopy="fun()" value="Please Copy Me!">
<script>    // run a JavaScript function
function fun(){ alert("The text has been copied") }
</script>
```

// Output: Please Copy Me!

The text has been copied"

---

oncuechange syntax:

<track oncuechange="function()" />

// Run a JavaScript function when the cue changes in a <track> element.

// About <track> element, please see <track> syntax.

e.g.

```
<video width="300" height="200" controls>
<source src="myVideo.mp4" type="video/mp4">
<track src="trk.vtt" kind="captions" srclang="en" label="English"
oncuechange="alert('The cue changes!')">
</video>
```

// Output: The cue changes!

---

oncut syntax:

<element type="" oncut="function()">

// Run function() when the content of the element is cut.

e.g.

```
<input type="text" oncut="fun()" value="Please Cut Me!">
<script>    // run a JavaScript function
function fun(){ alert("The text has been cut") }
</script>
```

// Output: Please Cut Me!

The text has been cut"

---

ondblclick syntax:

<element ondblclick="function()">

// Run function() when the element is double clicked.

e.g.

```
<button ondblclick="fun()">Double Click Me</button>
<script>    // run a JavaScript function
function fun(){ alert("The button is double clicked!"); }
```

```
</script>
// Output:   [Double Click Me]

The button is double clicked!
```

---

ondrag syntax:

```
<element ondrag="function()">
// Run function() when the content of the element is dragged.
e.g.
<p ondrag="fun()"> Highlight me and drag me! </p>
<script>    // run a JavaScript function
function fun(){ document.write("The text is dragged!"); }
</script>
// Output:   The text is dragged!
```

---

ondragend syntax:

```
<element ondragend="function()">
// Run function() when the content of an element has finished dragging.
e.g.
<p ondragend="fun()"> Highlight me and drag me! </p>
<script>    // run a JavaScript function
function fun(){ document.write("The text has finished dragging!"); }
</script>
// Output:   The text has finished dragging!
```

---

ondragenter syntax:

```
<element ondragenter="function(event)">
// Run function(event) when a draggable element enters a drop target.
// "ondragenter" needs to work with the complex JavaScript code.
// We do not study the complex JavaScript code in this book.
// To learn more "ondragenter", please reference JavaScript function,
JavaScript event, JavaScript library and JavaScript dom......
```

---

ondragleave syntax:

```
<element ondragleave="function()">
// Run function() when a draggable element leaves a drop target.
e.g.
<p ondragleave="fun()"> Highlight me and drag me! </p>
<script>    // run a JavaScript function
function fun(){ document.write("Leave the drop target!"); }
</script>
// Output:   Leave the drop target!
```

---

ondragover syntax:

```
<element ondragover="function(event)">
// Run function(event) when a draggable element is being dragged over a drop
target.
// "ondragover" needs to work with the complex JavaScript code.
// We do not study the complex JavaScript code in this book.
```

// To learn more "ondragover", please reference JavaScript function, JavaScript event, JavaScript library and JavaScript dom......

---

ondragstart syntax:

<element ondragstart="function()">

// Run function() when the content of an element starts to be dragged.

e.g.

```
<p ondragstart="fun()"> Highlight me and drag me! </p>
<script>     // run a JavaScript function
function fun(){ document.write("The text starts to be dragged!"); }
</script>
```

// Output: The text starts to be dragged!

---

ondrop syntax:

<element ondrop="function(event)">

// Run function(event) when a draggable element is dropped into a valid drop target.

// "ondrop" needs to work with the complex JavaScript code.

// We do not study the complex JavaScript code in this book.

// To learn more "ondrop", please reference JavaScript function, JavaScript event, JavaScript library and JavaScript dom......

---

ondurationchange syntax:

<audio controls ondurationchange="function()">

<video controls ondurationchange="function()">

// Run function() when the media duration changes

e.g.

```
<audio controls ondurationchange="fun(this)">
<source src="myMusic.mp3" type="audio/mpeg">
</audio>
<script>
function fun(m){   // "this" means the current  media object.
alert("The duration of this music is: " + m.duration/60 + " minutes");
}    // m.duration/60 returns the music duration in minutes
</script>
```

// Output: The duration of this music is: 3.688 minutes

---

onemptied syntax:

<audio controls onemptied="function()">

<video controls onemptied="function()">

// Run function() when media file or playlist is empty.

e.g.

```
<audio controls onemptied="fun()">
<source src="myMusic.mp3" type="audio/mpeg">
</audio>
<script>    // assume that the audio playlist is empty currently
function fun(){
alert("Audio playlist is empty!");
}
</script>
```

```
// Output:   Audio playlist is empty!
```

---

onended syntax:

```
<audio controls onended="function()">
<video controls onended="function()">
// Run function() when media has reached the end.
e.g.
<audio controls onended="fun()">
<source src="myMusic.mp3" type="audio/mpeg">
</audio>
<script>    // assume that the music has finished playing now
function fun(){
alert("The music has finished playing!");
}
</script>
// Output:   The music has finished playing!
```

---

onerror syntax:

```
<element onerror="function()">
// Run function() when an error occurs.
e.g.
<img src="image.jpg" onerror="fun()">
<script>
function fun(){ alert('Error! The image is not found!');}
</script>
// Output:   Error! The image is not found!
```

---

onfocus syntax:

```
<element type="" id="" onfocus="function()">
// Run function() when an element is focused.
e.g.
Name:<input type="text" id="n" onfocus="fun()">
<script>  // run a JavaScript function when inside text field is clicked
function fun(){alert("The text field is focused!");}
</script>
// Output:     Name:[              ]

                    The text field is focused!
```

---

onhashchange syntax:

```
<body onhashchange="function()">
// Run function() when the anchor part has been changed. The anchor part
starts with '#' symbol of the url. (www.example.com/xx.htm#part2)
// Using "location.hash" can change the anchor part.
e.g.
<body onhashchange="fun()">
<button onclick="anchorPart()">Change Anchor Part</button>
<script>
// change the anchor part by setting location.hash
function anchorPart() {
```

```
location.hash = "part2";   // change anchor part
}
function fun() {
alert("The anchor part has been changed to #part2");
}
</script>
</body>
```
// Output: The anchor part has been changed to #part2

---

oninput syntax:

<element type="" oninput="function()">

// Run function() when an element gets data from user input.

e.g.

```
<input type="text" id="xx" oninput="fun()">
<script>
function fun(){ alert("You have inputted data!"); }
</script>
```
// Output: You have inputted data!

---

oninvalid syntax:

<element type="" oninvalid="function()" required>

// Run function() when the element is invalid.

e.g.

```
<form action="" method="post">
Name: <input type="text" oninvalid="alert('The form cannot be empty!');" name="n" required>
<input type="submit" value="Submit">
</form>   // assume that we have submitted an empty form
```
// Output: The form cannot be empty!

---

onkeydown syntax:

<element type="" onkeydown="function()">

// Run function() when a key is down

e.g.

```
Text field: <input type="text" onkeydown="fun()">
<script>
function fun(){alert("A key is down in the text field!");
}
</script>
```
// Output: Text field: |

A key is down in the text field!

---

onkeypress syntax:

<element type="" onkeypress="function()">

// Run function() when a key is pressed

e.g.

```
Text field: <input type="text" onkeypress="fun()">
<script>
function fun(){alert("A key is pressed in the text field!");
```

```
}
</script>
```

// Output: Text field: p

A key is pressed in the text field!

---

onkeyup syntax:

```
<element type="" onkeyup="function()">
```

// Run function() when a key is up

e.g.

```
Text field: <input type="text" onkeyup="fun()">
<script>
function fun(){alert("A key is up in the text field!");
}
</script>
```

// Output: Text field: u

A key is up in the text field!

---

onload syntax:

```
<element onload="function()">
```

// Run function() when the element is loaded.

e.g.

```
<body onload="fun()">
Hello World!
<script>
function fun(){ alert("The webpage is loaded"); }
</script>
</body>
```

// Output: Hello World! The webpage is loaded

---

onloadeddata syntax:

```
<audio controls onloadeddata="function()"></audio>
<video controls onloadeddata="function()"></video>
```

// Run function() when the media data is loaded.

e.g.

```
<audio controls onloadeddata="fun()">
<source src="myMusic.mp3" type="audio/mpeg">
</audio>
<script>
function fun(){alert("Media data is loaded");}
</script>
```

// Output:

Media data is loaded

---

onloadedmetadata syntax:

```
<audio controls onloadedmetadata="function()"></audio>
<video controls onloadedmetadata="function()"></video>
// Run function() when the media meta data is loaded.
// "Media meta data" refers to text tracks, dimensions, and durations.
e.g.
<audio controls onloadedmetadata="fun()">
<source src="myMusic.mp3" type="audio/mpeg">
</audio>
<script>
function fun(){ alert("Media meta data is loaded"); }
</script>
// Output:   Media meta data is loaded
```

---

onloadstart syntax:

```
<audio controls onloadstart="function()"></audio>
<video controls onloadstart="function()"></video>
// Run function() when the media starts to load.
e.g.
<audio controls onloadstart="fun()">
<source src="myMusic.mp3" type="audio/mpeg">
</audio>
<script>
function fun(){ alert("Media starts to load"); }
</script>
// Output:   Media starts to load
```

---

onmousedown syntax:

```
<element onmousedown="function()">
// Run function() when the mouse is clicked down on an element.
e.g.
<h3 onmousedown="fun()">
Please click mouse down on me!
</h3>
<script>
function fun(){
alert("The mouse is clicked down on the text");
}
</script>
 // Output:   Please click mouse down on me!

 The mouse is clicked down on the text
```

---

onmousemove syntax:

```
<element onmousemove="function()">
// Run function() when the mouse is moved on an element.
e.g.
<h3 onmousemove="fun()">
Please move mouse on me!
</h3>
<script>
```

```
function fun(){
alert("The mouse is moved on the text");
}
</script>
```

// Output: **Please move mouse on me!**

The mouse is moved on the text

---

onmouseout syntax:

<element onmouseout="function()">

// Run function() when the mouse is shifted out of an element.

e.g.

```
<h3 onmouseout="fun()">
Please shift mouse out of me!
</h3>
<script>
function fun(){
alert("The mouse is shifted out of the text");
}
</script>
```

// Output: **Please shift mouse out of me!**

The mouse is shifted out of the text

---

onmouseover syntax:

<element onmouseover="function()">

// Run function() when the mouse hovers over an element.

e.g.

```
<h3 onmouseover="fun()">
Please hover the mouse over me!
</h3>
<script>
function fun(){
alert("The mouse hovers over the text");
}
</script>
```

// Output: **Please hover the mouse over me!**

The mouse hovers over the text

---

onmouseup syntax:

<element onmouseup="function()">

// Run function() when the mouse button is released up on an element.

e.g.

```
<h3 onmouseup="fun()">
Please click on me and release up the button!
</h3>
<script>
function fun(){
alert("The mouse button is released up on the text");
```

```
}
</script>
```
// Output: **Please click on me and release up the button!**

The mouse button is released up on the text

---

onmousewheel syntax:

<element onmousewheel="function()">

// Run function() when the mouse wheel is rolled over an element.

e.g.

```
<h3 onmousewheel="fun()">
Please roll the mouse wheel over me!
</h3>
<script>
function fun(){
alert("The mouse wheel is rolled over the text");
}
</script>
```
// Output: **Please roll the mouse wheel over me!**

The mouse wheel is rolled over the text

---

onpagehide syntax:

<body onpagehide="function()">

// Run function() when the page is going to hide.

// Note: Because of browser versions or settings, "onpagehide" event might not always work as we expected. It's not recommended to use.

e.g.

```
<body onpagehide="fun()">
<p>"onpagehide" event might not always work.</p>
<script>
function fun(){ alert("See You!"); }
</script>
</body>
```
// Output: "onpagehide" event might not always work. See You!

---

onpageshow syntax:

<body onpageshow="function()">

// Run function() when the page is going to show

e.g.

```
<body onpageshow="fun()">
Hello World!
<script>
function fun(){ alert("Show the page!"); }
</script>
</body>
```
// Output: Show the page! Hello World!

---

onpaste syntax:

<element type="" onpaste="function()">

// Run function() when a user paste something.
e.g.

```
Please copy me!
<input type="text" onpaste="fun()" value="Paste here">
<script>
function fun() {
alert("Paste finished!");
}
</script>
```

// Output: Please copy me! [Paste here]

Paste finished!

---

onpause syntax:

<audio id="" controls onpause="function()">
<video id="" controls onpause="function()">

// Run function() when the audio/video is paused.
e.g.

```
<audio id="m" controls onpause="fun()">
  <source src="myMusic.mp3" type="audio/mpeg">
</audio>
<script>
function fun(){ alert("The music is paused!"); }
</script>
```

// Output: 

The music is paused!

---

onplay syntax:

<audio id="" controls onplay="function()">
<video id="" controls onplay="function()">

// Run function() when the audio/video is played.
e.g.

```
<audio id="m" controls onplay="fun()">
  <source src="myMusic.mp3" type="audio/mpeg">
</audio>
<script>
function fun(){ alert("The music is played!"); }
</script>
```

// Output: 

The music is played!

---

onplaying syntax:

<audio id="" controls onplaying="function()">
<video id="" controls onplaying="function()">

```
// Run function() when the audio/video is played.
e.g.
<audio id="m" controls onplaying="fun()">
 <source src="myMusic.mp3" type="audio/mpeg">
</audio>
<script>
function fun(){ alert("The music is played!"); }
</script>
```

// Output: 

The music is played!

---

onprogress syntax:

<audio id="" controls onprogress="function()">
<video id="" controls onprogress="function()">

```
// Run function() when the audio/video will be downloaded.
e.g.
<audio id="m" controls onprogress="fun()">
 <source src="myMusic.mp3" type="audio/mpeg">
</audio>
<script>
function fun(){ alert("The music will be downloaded!"); }
</script>
```

// Output: 

The music will be downloaded!

---

onratechange syntax:

<audio id="" controls onratechange="function()">
<video id="" controls onratechange="function()">

```
// Run function() when the playing speed of the media is changed.
e.g.
<video id="myVideo" controls onratechange="fun()">
<source src="myVideo.mp4" type="video/mp4">
</video><br>
<button onclick="playSpeed()" type="button">Play Slower</button>
<script>     // assume that we set the playing speed of video as 0.5
function playSpeed(){ myVideo.playbackRate = 0.5; }
function fun(){ alert("The playing speed of the video is changed!"); }
</script>
```

// Output:

Play Slower   The playing speed of the video is changed!

---

onreset syntax:

```
<form onreset="function()">
```

// Run function() when the form is reset.

e.g.

```
<form onreset="fun()">
Name: <input type="text">
<input type="reset">
</form>
<script>
function fun(){ alert("The form has been reset!"); }
</script>
```

// Output: 

The form has been reset!

---

onresize syntax:

```
<body onresize="function()">
```

// Run function() when the browser window is resized.

e.g.

```
<body onresize="fun()">
<p>Please resize the browser window.</p>
<script>
function fun(){ alert("The browser window changes!");}
</script>
</body>
```

// Output: Please resize the browser window.
The browser window changes!

---

onscroll syntax:

```
<element onscroll="function()">
```

// Run function() when the scrollbar of the element is scrolled.

e.g.

```
<textarea onscroll="fun()">
AAA
BBB
CCC
DDD
EEE
FFF
</textarea>
<script>
function fun(){ alert("The scrollbar is scrolled!");}
</script>
```

// Output: The scrollbar is scrolled!

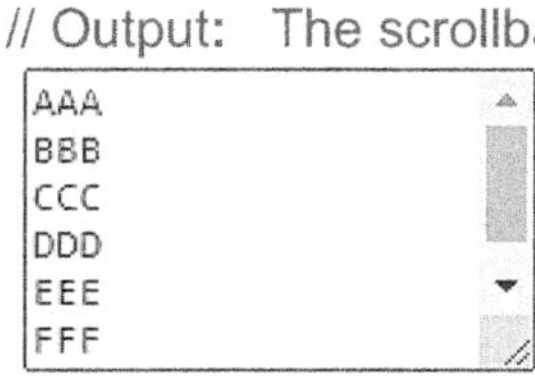

----

onsearch syntax:

```
<input type="search" id="" onsearch="function()">
```

// Run function() when a user enters data into search filed.

e.g.

```
Enter searching keywords:
<input type="search" id="sch" onsearch="fun()">
<script>
function fun(){ alert( "You are searching: " + sch.value);}
</script>
```

// Output: Enter searching keywords: Hello

You are searching: Hello

----

onseeked syntax:

```
<audio id="" controls onseeked="function()">
<video id="" controls onseeked="function()">
```

// Run function() when the media's progress bar has been adjusted.

e.g.

```
<audio controls onseeked="fun()">
<source src="myMusic.mp3" type="audio/mpeg">
</audio>
<script>
function fun(){ alert("The music has been skipped");}
</script>
```

// Output: 

The music has been skipped!

----

onseeking syntax:

```
<audio id="" controls onseeking="function()">
<video id="" controls onseeking="function()">
```

// Run function() when the media's progress bar is being adjusted.

e.g.

```
<audio controls onseeking="fun()">
<source src="myMusic.mp3" type="audio/mpeg">
</audio>
<script>
function fun(){ alert("The music is being skipped");}
</script>
```

// Output: 

The music is being skipped!

----

onselect syntax:

```
<element type="" value="" onselect="function()">
```

// Run function() when the element content is selected or highlighted.

e.g.

```
<input type="text" value="Highlight Me" onselect="fun()">
<script>
function fun(){ alert("The text is being highlighting!"); }
</script>
// Output:    Highlight Me
```

The text is being highlighting!

---

onstalled syntax:

```
<audio id="" controls onstalled="function()">
<video id="" controls onstalled="function()">
// Run function() when the media data is not available.
// Note: Because of browser versions or settings, "onstalled" event might not always work as we expected.
e.g.
<audio controls onstalled="fun()">
<source src="myMusic.mp3" type="audio/mpeg">
</audio>
<script>
function fun(){ alert("The music data is not available!");}
</script>
// Output:    ▶ 0:00 / 0:00
```

The music data is not available!

---

onsubmit syntax:

```
<form action="" id="" onsubmit="function()">
// Run function() when a form is submitted
e.g.
<form action="" id="" onsubmit="fun()">
Name: <input type="text" name="n">
<input type="submit" value="Submit">
</form>
<script>
function fun(){ alert("The form is submitted!");}
</script>
</body>
// Output:    Name: hello  Submit
```

The form is submitted!

---

onsuspend syntax:

```
<audio id="" controls onsuspend="function()">
<video id="" controls onsuspend="function()">
// Run function() when the media is suspended after page is refreshed.
e.g.
<audio controls onsuspend="fun()">
<source src="myMusic.mp3" type="audio/mpeg">
</audio>
```

```
<script>  // during the music is playing, please refresh the webpage
function fun(){ alert("The music is suspended!");}
</script>
```

// Output: 

The music is suspended!

---

ontimeupdate syntax:

```
<audio id="" controls ontimeupdate="function()">
<video id="" controls ontimeupdate="function()">
```

// Run function() when the playing time of the media is being updated.

e.g.

```
<audio controls ontimeupdate="fun()">
<source src="myMusic.mp3" type="audio/mpeg">
</audio>
<script>
function fun(){ alert("The playing time of the media is being updated!");}
</script>
```

// Output: 

The playing time of the media is being updated!

---

ontoggle syntax:

```
<details ontoggle="function()">
```

// Run function() when a user opens or closes a <details> element.

e.g.

```
<details ontoggle="fun()">
<summary>About Cantonese Language</summary>
<p>Cantonese is a language with a history of thousands of years, it is spoken
in Canton, Hong Kong, Macau, and Southern area of China.</p>
</details>
<script>
function fun(){ alert("The ontoggle action happens!");}
</script>
```

// Output: ▼ About Cantonese Language

The ontoggle action happens!

---

onunload syntax:

```
<body onunload="function()">
```

// Run function() when a page is unload.

// Note: Because of browser versions or settings, "onunload" event might not always work as we expected. It's not recommended to use.

e.g.

```
<body onunload="fun()">
<p>"onunload" event might not always work.</p>
<script>
function fun() { alert(" See You! "); }
</script>
```

```
</body>
// Output:    "onunload" event might not always work.      See You!
```

---

onvolumechange syntax:

```
<audio controls  onvolumechange="function()">
<video controls  onvolumechange="function()">
// Run function() when the volume of a media is being changed
e.g.
<audio controls  onvolumechange="fun()">
 <source src="myMusic.mp3" type="audio/mpeg" />
 </audio>
 <script>
  function fun(){ alert("The volume is being changed!"); }
 </script>
```

// Output:

The volume is being changed!

---

onwaiting syntax:

```
<audio controls onwaiting="function()">
<video controls onwaiting="function()">
// Run function() when the media needs to buffer and stop playing due to a
temporary lack of media data.
e.g.
<video controls onwaiting="fun()">
<source src="myVideo.mp4" type="video/mp4">
</video>
<script>
function fun(){ alert("Wait! The video is buffering!"); }
</script>
// Output:   Wait! The video is buffering!
```

---

onwheel syntax:

```
<element onwheel="function()">
// Run function() when the mouse wheel is rolled over an element.
e.g.
<h3 onwheel="fun()">
Please roll the mouse wheel over me!
</h3>
<script>
function fun(){
alert("The mouse wheel is rolled over the text");
}
</script>
```

// Output: **Please roll the mouse wheel over me!**

The mouse wheel is rolled over the text

---

open syntax:

<details open>

// Specify the detailed contents must be open by default

e.g.

```
<details open>
<summary>About Cantonese Language</summary>
<p>Cantonese is a language with a history of thousands of years, it is spoken in Canton, Hong Kong, Macau, and Southern area of China.</p>
</details>
```

// Output: ▼ About Cantonese Language

Cantonese is a language with a history of thousands of years, it is spoken in Canton, Hong Kong, Macau, and Southern area of China.

---

optimum syntax:

<meter id="" value="" high="" low="" optimum="value"></meter>

// Specify the optimum value in a meter

e.g.

```
<label for="mt">Meter:</label>
<meter id="mt" value="0.6" high="0.8" low="0.1" optimum="0.5"></meter> // indicate that "0.5" is the optimum value
```

// Output: Meter: 

---

padding style syntax:

padding: value

// The padding is the area around the text content in a content box.

// The padding width can be specified with a padding attribute.

e.g.

```
<style type = "text/css">
#b1{border-style: solid;  border-width: 5px; padding: 10px }
#b2{border-style: dotted;  border-width: 5px; padding: 20px }
</style>
<p id = "b1">This padding is 10px.</p>
<p id = "b2">This padding is 20px.</p>
```

// Output:

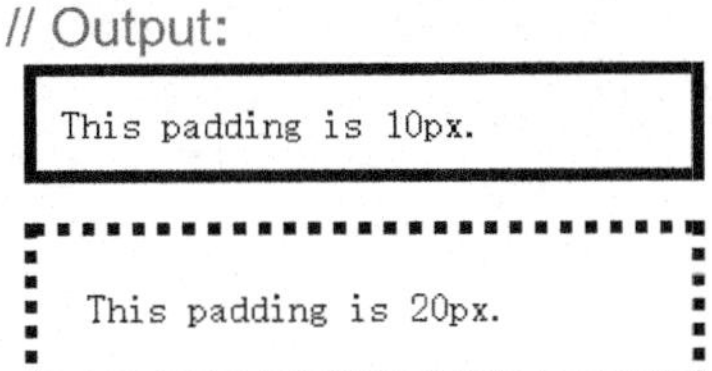

---

password type syntax:

<input type="password" name="user-password">

// The password type in HTML is used for input fields where the user enters sensitive information, like a password.

e.g.

```
<p>Enter your password:</p>
  <form>
    <input type="password" id="password" name="password">
    <input type="submit" value="Submit">
  </form>
```

// Output: Enter your password:

[ ] Submit

---

pattern syntax:

<input type="" id="" pattern="regular_expression">

// Specify a regular expression which validates the inputted data of form.

e.g.

```
<form action="">
<p>Please enter 4-bits pin number:</p>
<input type="password" id="pin" pattern="[0-9]{4}">
<input type="submit">
</form>
```

// Output: Please enter 4-bits pin number:

[ ] Submit

---

pause() syntax:

video_id.pause()

// Pause video according to the video id.

e.g.

```
<button onclick="fun1()" type="button">Play Video</button>
<button onclick="fun2()" type="button">Pause Video</button><br>
<video id="vid" width="300" height="180">
  <source src="myVideo.mp4" type="video/mp4">
</video>
<script>
function fun1(){vid.play();}
function fun2(){vid.pause();}
</script>
```

// Output:

Play Video | Pause Video

---

paused syntax:

video_id.paused

// Return true if the video is paused, return false if the video is playing.

e.g.

```
<button onclick="fun()" type="button">Check Paused</button><br>
<video id="v" width="300" height="180" controls>
  <source src="myVideo.mp4" type="video/mp4">
</video>
<script>
function fun(){ alert( "Is the video paused? " + v.paused); }
</script>    // assume that the video has been paused currently.
```

// Output: [Check Paused] Is the video paused? true

---

placeholder syntax:

```
<input type="" id="" placeholder="short_hint">
<textarea id="" placeholder="short_hint">
```

// "placeholder" specifies a short hint in an input field or a textarea.

e.g.

```
<form action="myFile.php">   // php file processes the inputted data
Please enter a telephone number: <br>
<input type="tel" id="phone" placeholder="012-345-6789"
pattern="[0-9]{3}-[0-9]{3}-[0-9]{4}" required>
<input type="submit">
</form>
```

// Output: Please enter a telephone number:

[012-345-6789] [Submit]

---

play() syntax:

```
video_id.play()
```

// Play video according to the video id.

e.g.

```
<button onclick="fun1()" type="button">Play Video</button>
<button onclick="fun2()" type="button">Pause Video</button><br>
<video id="vid" width="300" height="180">
  <source src="myVideo.mp4" type="video/mp4">
</video>
<script>
function fun1(){vid.play();}
function fun2(){vid.pause();}
</script>
```

// Output:

[Play Video] [Pause Video]

---

played syntax:

```
id.played.start(0)   // return the start of the video played range
id.played.end(0)   // return the end of the video played range
```

e.g.

```
<button onclick="fun()" type="button">Played Range</button><br>
<video id="vid" width="300" height="180" controls>
<source src="myVideo.mp4" type="video/mp4">
</video>
<script>
function fun() {
alert("Start: " + vid.played.start(0) + " End: "  + vid.played.end(0));
}    // (0) means the first video, if there are multiple videos in a page.
</script>
```

// Output: [Played Range]   Start: 0   End: 38.680659

---

position absolute syntax:

position: absolute; top: value; left: value

// "position: absolute" sets the precise location of the contents.
// "top: value" sets the distance from the top edge of the window.
// "left: value" sets the distance from the left edge of the window.

e.g.

```
<style type = "text/css">
#a1{ position:absolute; top: 0px; left: 30px }
#a2{ position:absolute; top: 30px; left: 60px }
</style>
<p id = "a1">This is position1.</p>
<p id = "a2">This is position2.</p>
```

// Output:

This is position1.

This is position2.

---

position relative syntax:

position: relative; top: percentage; left: percentage

// "position: relative" sets the relative location of the contents based on the browser window resolution or window size.
// "top: percentage" sets the distance from the top edge of the window.
// "left: percentage" sets the distance from the left edge of the window.

e.g.

```
<style type = "text/css">
#r{ position:relative; top: 3%; left: 5% }
</style>
<p id = "r">This is the relative position.</p>
```

// Output:

This is the relative position.

---

poster syntax:

<video width="" height="" poster="image.jpg" controls>

// Poster an image when loading a video.
// The image will not disappear until the video is played.

e.g.

```
<video  width="210" height="140" poster="flower.jpg" controls>
<source src="myVideo.mp4" type="video/mp4">
</video>
```

// Output:

---

preload syntax:

<audio controls preload="auto/metadata/none">
<video controls preload="auto/metadata/none">
// "auto": Loads the entire audio/video when the page loads.
// "metadata": Only loads media metadata when the page loads.
// "none": Do not preload the audio/video when the page loads.
e.g.

```
<audio controls preload="none">
<source src="myMusic.mp3" type="audio/mpeg">
</audio>
```

// Output: 

---

preload syntax:

video_id.preload="auto/none/metadata" // set how to preload video
video_id.preload // return the preloading status of the video
// "auto" sets to preload the video, "none" sets not to preload the video.
// "metadata" sets to preload the metadata of video only.
e.g.

```
<button onclick="fun1()" type="button">Auto Preload</button>
<button onclick="fun2()" type="button">None Preload</button>
<button onclick="fun3()" type="button">Check Preload</button><br>
<video id="v" width="300" height="180" controls>
  <source src="myVideo.mp4" type="video/mp4">
</video>
<script>
function fun1(){ v.preload = "auto"; }
function fun2(){ v.preload = "none"; }
function fun3(){ alert( "Preload Status? " + v.preload); }
</script>  // assume that we click "Auto Preload" and "Check Preload".
```

// Output: [Auto Preload] [None Preload] [Check Preload] Preload Status? auto

---

putImageData() syntax:

ctx.putImageData(imageData, x, y);
// Paints pixel data from an ImageData object onto the canvas.
// x, y: The coordinates on the canvas where the top-left corner of the ImageData object will be placed.
e.g.

```
<canvas id="myCanvas" width="150" height="150"></canvas>
<script>
  const canvas = document.getElementById('myCanvas');
  const ctx = canvas.getContext('2d');
```

```
  // Draw a green rectangle on the canvas
  ctx.fillStyle = "green";
  ctx.fillRect(20, 20, 50, 50);
  // Get the ImageData for the green rectangle
  let imageData = ctx.getImageData(20, 20, 50, 50);
  // Put the ImageData (green rectangle) back at a different location
  ctx.putImageData(imageData, 80, 80);
</script>
// Output:
```

---

radio type syntax:

<input type="radio" name="group-name">

// Used with the <input> element to create radio buttons, allowing users to select one option from a set of predefined choices. Only one radio button in a group can be selected at a time.

e.g.

```
<form>
  <p>Select your favorite fruit:</p>
  <input type="radio" id="apple" name="fruit" value="apple">
  <label for="apple">apple</label><br>
  <input type="radio" id="banana" name="fruit" value="banana">
  <label for="banana">banana</label><br>
  <input type="radio" id="cherry" name="fruit" value="cherry">
  <label for="cherry">cherry</label>
</form>
```

// Output: Select your favorite fruit:

◉ apple
○ banana
○ cherry

---

range type syntax:

<input type="range" id="..." name="..." min="..." max="..." step="...">

// This is used with the <input> element to create a slider control, allowing users to select a value from a given range.
// The min attribute sets the minimum allowed value.
// The max attribute sets the maximum allowed value.
// The step attribute specifies the increments.

```
<form>
  <label for="volume">Volume Range:</label>
  <input type="range" id="volume" name="volume" min="0" max="100">
</form>
```

e.g.

// Output: Volume Range: 

---

readonly syntax;

<input type="" id="" value="" readonly>

<textarea id="" value="" readonly>

// Specify a default read-only value for the element

e.g.

```
<form action="">
Name: <input type="text"><br>
* Age: <input type="number" value="18" readonly><br>
Only 18 years old allowed: <input type="submit" value="Submit">
</form>
```

// Output:

Name: [ ]

* Age: [18]

Only 18 years old allowed: [Submit]

---

readyState syntax:

media_id.readyState

// Get a ready state number of a media. The ready state number is:

"0"	no information about the audio/video available.
"1"	only metadata available.
"2"	only the current data available, but next data unavailable.
"3"	the current data and next data available, but not enough.
"4"	all data available to start playing.

e.g.

```
<button onclick="fun()" type="button">Get Ready State</button><br>
<video id="v" width="300" height="180" controls>
<source src="myVideo.mp4" type="video/mp4">
</video>
<script>
function fun() { alert("The current ready state is " + v.readyState);}
</script>
```

// Output: [Get Ready State] The current ready state is 4

---

rect() syntax:

rect(x, y, width, height)

// Create a rectangle by specifying its position and dimensions.

// x: The x-coordinate of the rectangle's starting point (top-left corner).

// y: The y-coordinate of the rectangle's starting point (top-left corner).

e.g.

```
<canvas id="myCanvas" width="150" height="100"></canvas>
  <script>
    var ctx = document.getElementById('myCanvas').getContext('2d');
    ctx.rect(20, 20, 100, 50);   // Draw a rectangle
    ctx.stroke();   // Outline the rectangle
  </script>
```

// Output:

---

rel syntax:

<element rel="value" href="">

// Specify the relationship between the current page and the linked page.
// About the "rel value", please see the "Rel Values Chart" in Appendix.

e.g.

<a **rel="nofollow"**
href="http://mybook.to/yaowining">Ray Yao's website</a>
// Output: Ray Yao's website

---

required syntax:

<element type="" required>
<select required>
<textarea required>

// Specify that data must be provided before the form can be submitted

e.g.

<form action="" method="post">
<input type="text" oninvalid="alert('Form can't be empty!');" **required**>
<input type="submit" value="Submit">
</form> // assume that we have submitted an empty form
// Output: Form can't be empty!

---

reset type syntax:

<input type="reset" value="Reset">

// Used with the <input> element to create a button that resets all the form fields to their initial values when clicked.

e.g.

<form>
<label for="name">Enter your name:</label>
<input type="text" id="name" name="name">
<input **type="reset"** value="Reset">
</form>
// Output: Enter your name: [ ] [Reset]

---

reversed syntax:

<ol reversed> </ol>

// Specify that the numbers of the <ol> list must be descending.

e.g.

<ol **reversed**>
<li>Apple</li>
<li>Banana</li>
<li>Cherry</li>
</ol>
// Output:

3. Apple
2. Banana
1. Cherry

---

rotate() syntax:

context.rotate(angle);

// Used to rotate the entire canvas around its current origin by a specified angle. The angle is measured in radians, and the rotation is clockwise. To rotate counterclockwise, use a negative angle.

e.g.

```
<canvas id="myCanvas" width="120" height="120" style="border:1px solid black;"></canvas>
  <script>
    var ctx = document.getElementById('myCanvas').getContext('2d');
    ctx.translate(60, 60);    // Translate to the center of the canvas
    ctx.rotate(Math.PI / 4);    // Rotate the canvas by 45 degrees (in radians)
    ctx.fillStyle = "red";    // Draw a rectangle after rotation
    ctx.fillRect(-25, -25, 50, 50);    // Center the rectangle at the origin
  </script>
```

// Output:

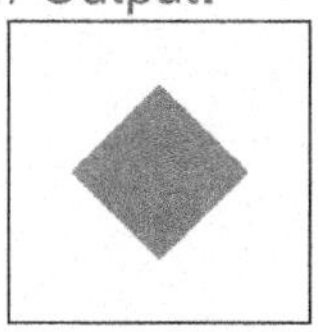

----

rows syntax:

<textarea rows="" cols="">

// Specify the height of a text area.

e.g.

```
<textarea rows="3" cols="40">
About the size of this textarea:
The row of this textarea is 3
The cols of this textarea is 20
</textarea>
```

// Output:

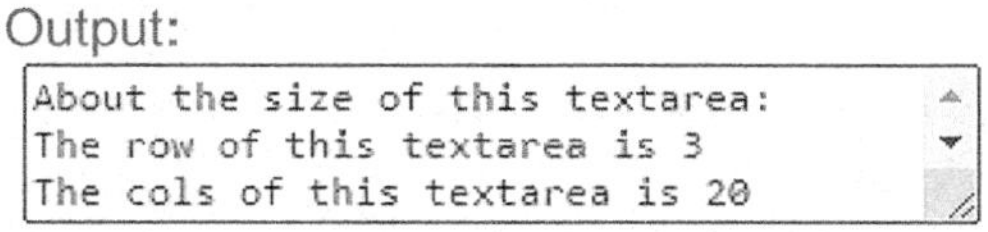

----

rowspan syntax:

<td width="" rowspan="" colspan="">

// "width" sets the width of a cell

// "rowspan" sets the numbers of rows to span across.

// "colspan" sets the numbers of column to span across.

e.g.

```
<table border = "1" >
<tr>
<td width=100 rowspan = 2>Cell 1</td>
<td>Cell 2</td><td>Cell 3</td>
</tr>
<tr>
<td>Cell 5</td><td>Cell 6</td>
</tr>
</table>
```

// Output:

Cell 1	Cell 2	Cell 3

	Cell 5	Cell 6

---

sandbox allowed syntax:

```
<iframe src="" sandbox="value"> </iframe>
<iframe srcdoc="" sandbox="value"> </iframe>
// Specify an allowed value to the <iframe> content by sandbox.
// Please see "Sandbox Allowed Value Chart" in Appendix.
<iframe srcdoc="<script>document.write('Script is allowed!')</script>"
 sandbox="allow-scripts">    // allow to run javascript
</iframe>
// Output:
```

Script is allowed!

---

sandbox restriction syntax:

```
<iframe src="" sandbox> </iframe>
<iframe srcdoc="" sandbox="value"> </iframe>
// Specify a group of restrictions to the <iframe> content by sandbox.
// Please see "Sandbox Restricted Value Chart" in Appendix.
e.g.
<iframe  src = "myVideo.mp4" sandbox> </iframe>
// The video cannot be played automatically after using "sandbox"
// Output:
```

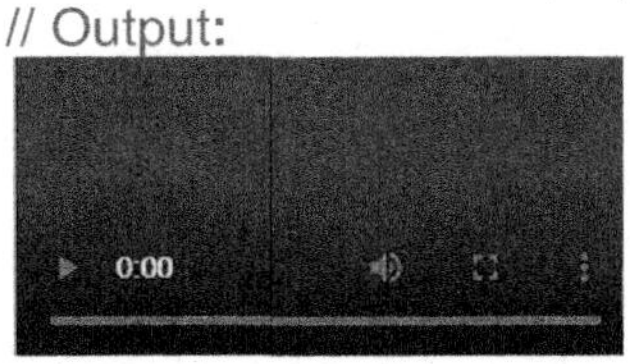

---

scale() syntax:

```
context.scale(x, y);
// Scale the current drawing, resizing it horizontally by x and vertically by y.
// x: Scaling factor in the horizontal direction.
// y: Scaling factor in the vertical direction.
e.g.
<canvas id="myCanvas" width="150" height="150" style="border:1px solid black;"></canvas>
  <script>
    var ctx = document.getElementById('myCanvas').getContext('2d');
    ctx.fillStyle = "green";    // Draw a rectangle without scaling
    ctx.fillRect(10, 10, 50, 50);
    ctx.scale(2, 2);    // Double size in both directions by scaling
      ctx.fillStyle = "red";    // Draw a rectangle after scaling
    ctx.fillRect(10, 10, 50, 50);
  </script>
// Output:
```

----

scope syntax:

<th scope="row/rowgroup"> // set a row or rowgroup as a header
<th scope="col/colgroup"> // set a col or colgroup as a header

e.g.

```
<table border="1">
<tr><th scope="col">A</th><th colspan="3" scope="colgroup">B</th></tr>
<tr><td>1</td><td>2</td><td>3</td><td>4</td></tr>
</table>
```

// Output:

A	B		
1	2	3	4

----

search type syntax:

<input type="search" name="search-query">

// This is used for input fields specifically designed for search queries.

e.g.

```
<p>Search the site:</p>
   <form>
      <input type="search" id="search" name="search-query"
placeholder="Search...">
      <input type="submit" value="Go">
   </form>
```

// Output: Search the site:

[Search...] [Go]

----

seekable syntax:

id.seekable.start(0) // return the start of the video seekable range
id.seekable.end(0) // return the end of the video seekable range

// "seekable range": a media range that is available for seeking by user.

e.g.

```
<button onclick="fun()" type="button">Seekable Range</button><br>
<video id="vid" width="300" height="180" controls>
<source src="myVideo.mp4" type="video/mp4">
</video>
<script>
function fun() {
alert("Start: " + vid.seekable.start(0) + " End: " + vid.seekable.end(0));
}   // (0) means the first video, if there are multiple videos in a page.
</script>
```

// Output: [Seekable Range] Start: 0 End: 59.992

----

selected syntax:

<option value="" selected>...</option>

// Specify that an option must be pre-selected when the page is loaded.

e.g.

```
<select name="mySelect">
   <option value="apple" selected>Apple</option>
   <option value="banana">Banana</option>
   <option value="cherry">Cherry</option>
</select>
```

// Output:

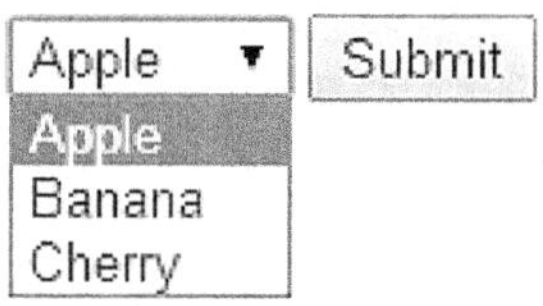

---

shape syntax:

<map>
<area shape="", coords="", href="", alt="">
</map>

// <map> defines an image map with clickable area.

// <area> defines a clickable area inside the image map, which can redirect to another specified page.

// "shape" specifies the shape of the area.

// "coords" specifies the coordinates of an area in an image map.

// "href" sets the url of the page. "alt" sets an alternate text.

e.g. please see the example of <map> syntax or <area> syntax.

---

size syntax:

<input size="number"> // set the max number of inputted characters

<select size="number"> // set the number of visible options

e.g.

```
Name: <input type="text" id="name" size="15"> // limit 15 characters
<input type="submit" value="Submit">
```

// Output:

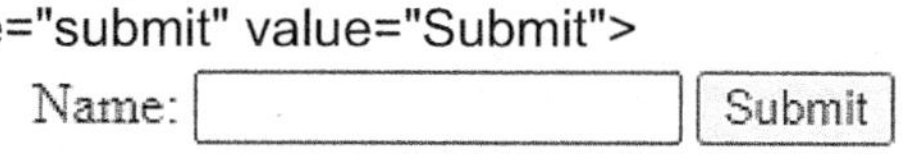

---

spacing syntax:

line-height // specify line spacing.

word-spacing // specify word spacing.

letter-spacing // specify letter spacing.

e.g.

```
<style type = "text/css">
#lineSpacing{ line-height:500% }
#wordSpacing{ word-spacing: 10px }
#letterSpacing{ letter-spacing: 5px }
</style>
<p id = "lineSpacing">Line Spacing Sample.</p>
<p id = "wordSpacing">Word Spacing Sample.</p>
<p id = "letterSpacing">Letter Spacing Sample.</p>
```

// Output:

Line Spacing Sample

Word   Spacing   Sample.
L e t t e r   S p a c I n g   S a m p l e.

----

span syntax:

<col span="number" style=" "> </col>
<colgroup span="number" style=" "> </colgroup>
// Specify a number to span columns for <col> or <colgroup> element.
e.g.
<table border="1">   // span="2" sets a number to span 2 columns
<colgroup **span="2"** style="background:yellow"></colgroup>
<tr><th>Col1</th><th>Col2</th><th>Col3</th></tr>
<tr><td>A</td><td>B</td><td>C</td></tr>
<tr><td>a</td><td>b</td><td>c</td></tr>
</table>
// Output:

Col1	Col2	Col3
A	B	C
a	b	c

----

spellcheck syntax:

<element spellcheck="true/false">
// Check grammatical or spelling mistakes in the text fields.
e.g.
<textarea **spellcheck="true"**>
This is a boook, it is the besst boook in the world!
</textarea>   // display red wavy lines under misspelling words.
// Output:

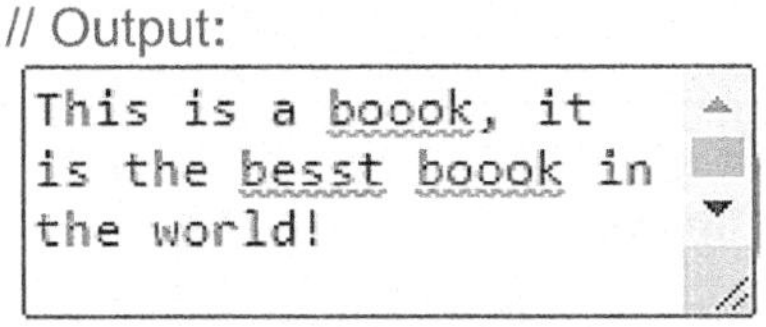

----

src syntax:

<element src = "" alt = "">
// "src" specifies an url of the external resource
// "alt" sets an alternate text.
e.g.
<img **src = "flower.jpg"** width = "100" height = "80"
alt = "This is a flower.">
// Output:

---

src syntax:

```
video_id.src = myVideo
// Set the current resource of an video
e.g.
<button onclick="fun()" type="button">Change Video</button><br>
<video id="vid" width="300" height="180" controls autoplay>
  <source  src="video1.mp4" type="video/mp4">
  <source  src="video2.mp4" type="video/mp4">
</video>
<script>
function fun() { vid.src = "video2.mp4"; vid.load(); }
</script>
// Output:
```

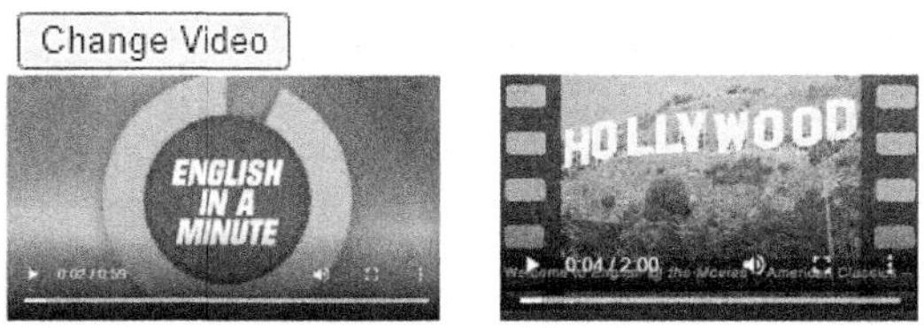

video1 video2

---

srcdoc syntax:

```
<iframe srcdoc="html_code"> </iframe>
// Specify to show the HTML content in the inline frame.
e.g.
<iframe srcdoc="<p>Hello world!</p>"> </iframe>
// Output:
```

Hello World!

---

srclang syntax:

```
<track src="" kind="" srclang="" label="" default>
// "srclang" specifies the language of the track text data.
// <track> defines subtitle, caption, description for <audio> or <video>.
// "src" specifies a track file. "kind" sets the subtitle, caption…
// "kind" specifies the kind of text track. It works with "srclang" together.
// "label" sets the title of the text track.
// "default" sets the track enabled unless user sets other preferences.
e.g.    See the example <track> syntax
```

---

srcset syntax:

```
<picture>
  <source media="..." srcset="…">
  <source media="..." srcset="…">
  <img src="...">
</picture>
// "srcset" specifies the url of different images.
```

// <picture> element is a container for two <source> elements and one <img> element. It allows to specify several images designed to better fill the browser viewport properly.
// The browser always displays the first <source> element whose image matches the current viewport width.
// "media" specifies the minimum width of the images.
e.g.

```
<picture>
<source media="(min-width:500px)"  srcset="flower1.jpg">
<source media="(min-width:700px)"  srcset="flower2.jpg">
<img src="flowers3.jpg"  alt="Flowers"  style="width:auto;">
</picture>
```

// Output:

---

start syntax:

<ol start="number"> </ol>
// Specify the first list number of the <ol> element.
e.g.

```
<ol start="28">
   <li>Apple</li>
   <li>Banana</li>
   <li>Cherry</li>
</ol>
```

// Output:

28. Apple
29. Banana
30. Cherry

---

step syntax:

<input type="number" step="number">
// Specify a number to represent its valid multiples.
// Example: if step="2", the valid multiples will be -2, 0, 2, 4, 6 etc.
e.g.

```
<form action="">
Enter a number that is a multiple of 5: <br>
  <input type="number" step="5">
  <input type="submit">
</form>
```

// Output: Enter a number that is a multiple of 5:
[15] [Submit]

---

stroke syntax:

stroke="color"
// Set the color of the stroke in svg
e.g.

```
<svg width="200" height="100">
```

```
<path stroke="red" d="M10,10 L100,10" />
</svg>   // about d="M10,10 L100,10", please see <path> syntax.
// Output:
```

---

stroke() syntax:

context.strokeTo();

// Draw a path with the moveTo() and lineTo() methods for canvas.

e.g.

```
<canvas id="cid" width="100" height="50" ></canvas>
<script>
var context = cid.getContext("2d");
context.moveTo(0, 0);
context.lineTo(100, 50);
context.stroke();
</script>
// Output:
```

---

stroke-dasharray syntax:

stroke-dasharray="dash-length, gap-length"

// Set the dash-array of the stroke in svg

e.g.

```
<svg width="200" height="100">
<path stroke="red" stroke-width="3" stroke-dasharray="8,6" d="M10,10
L100,10" />
</svg>   // about d="M10,10 L100,10", please see <path> syntax.
// Output:
```

---

stroke-linecap syntax:

stroke-linecap="butt / round / square"

// Set the line-cap of the stroke in svg

e.g.

```
<svg width="200" height="100">
<path stroke="red" stroke-width="20" stroke-linecap="round" d="M10,10
L100,10" />
</svg>   // about d="M10,10 L100,10", please see <path> syntax.
// Output:
```

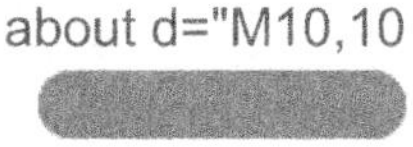

---

strokeRect() syntax:

strokeRect(x, y, width, height);

// Used to draw the outline of a rectangle, defined by its position, width, and height. It draws only the rectangle's border, without filling the interior.

// x: The x-coordinate of the rectangle's starting point (top-left corner).

// y: The y-coordinate of the rectangle's starting point.

e.g.

```
<canvas id="myCanvas" width="100" height="80" style="border:1px solid black;"></canvas>
  <script>
    // Get the canvas element and its context
```

```
    var canvas = document.getElementById('myCanvas');
    var ctx = canvas.getContext('2d');
    ctx.strokeStyle = "green";   // Set the stroke color
    ctx.strokeRect(10, 10, 80, 60);   // Draw the rectangle outline
  </script>
// Output:
```

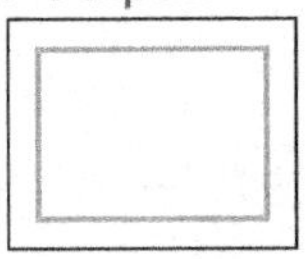

---

stroke-width syntax:

stroke-width="number"

// Set the width of the stroke in svg

e.g.

```
<svg width="200" height="100">
<path stroke="red" stroke-width="8" d="M10,10 L100,10" />
</svg>   // about d="M10,10 L100,10", please see <path> syntax.
// Output:
```

---

strokeStyle syntax

context.strokeStyle = color;

// Specifies the color, gradient, or pattern used to stroke shapes and lines.

e.g.

```
<canvas id="myCanvas" width="160" height="160" style="border:1px solid black;"></canvas>
  <script>
    var ctx = document.getElementById('myCanvas').getContext('2d');
    ctx.strokeStyle = "blue";   // Set the stroke color
    ctx.beginPath();   // Draw a rectangle with the specified stroke style
    ctx.rect(30, 30, 100, 100);
    ctx.stroke();
  </script>
// Output:
```

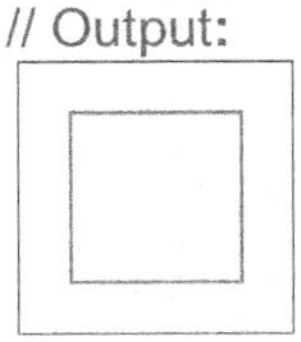

---

strokeText() syntax:

context.strokeText("text", x, y);

// Draw text without filled on the canvas. The text is black by default.

// "x" is the x- coordinate where to begin drawing the text

// "y" is the y- coordinate where to begin drawing the text

e.g.

```
<canvas id="cid" width="100" height="50"></canvas>
<script>
var context = cid.getContext("2d");   // return a canvas context
context.font = "15px Arial black";   // set a font
context.strokeText("Hello World", 5, 25);   // stroke text
```

</script>
// Output: Hello World

---

style (inline) syntax:

<element style = "attribute:value">……
// Define an inline style css.
// Apply the specified style to the tag and its content.
e.g.
<p **style =** "color: blue; font-family: Arial Black; font-size: 10pt"> Inline Sample </p>
// Output: **Inline Sample**

---

submit type syntax:

<input type="submit" value="Submit">
// Used with the <input> element to create a button that submits the form data when clicked.
e.g.
<form action="myfile.php">
<label for="name">Enter your name:</label>
<input type="text" id="name" name="name">
<input **type="submit"** value="Submit">
</form>
// Output: Enter your name: [ ] Submit

---

tabindex syntax:

<element tabindex="number">
// Specify the tab sequence number of an element so that a user can navigate the contents by pressing the "Tab" button.
e.g.
<p **tabindex="1"**>Apple</p> // please press "Tab" button to navigate
<p **tabindex="2"**>Banana</p>
<p **tabindex="3"**>Cherry</p>
// Output:
Apple
Banana
Cherry

---

target syntax:

< a / area / base / form target="_blank / _self / _parent / _top">
// "_blank": another new page will be opened in a new tab.
// "_self": a self page will be opened on its original window.
// "_parent": a target page will be opened in a parent frame.
// "_top": a target page will be opened in the topmost frame.
e.g.
<a href="http://www.amazon.com" **target="_self"**>To Amazon</a>
<a href="http://www.google.com" **target="_blank"**>To Google</a>
// Output: To Amazon To Google

---

tel type syntax:

<input type="tel" name="user-phone">

```
// This is used for input fields where user is expected to enter a phone number.
e.g.
<p>Enter your phone number:</p>
<form>
<input type="tel" id="phone" name="phone" placeholder="123-456-7890">
<input type="submit" value="Submit">
</form>
// Output:    Enter your phone number:
           123-456-7890  Submit
```

---

text type syntax:

<input type="text" name="username">

```
// Defines a single-line text input field. The default width of the text field is 20
characters.
e.g.
<form>
  <label>Please input your name: </label><br>
  <input type="text" id="myid" name="myname">
</form>
// Output:    Please input your name:
```

---

textMetrics syntax:

var textMetrics = context.measureText(text);

```
// Provides information about the dimensions of the text string that was
measured, including properties such as the width of the text.
e.g.
e.g.
<canvas id="myCanvas" width="200" height="80" style="border:1px solid black;"></canvas>
   <script>
      var canvas = document.getElementById('myCanvas');
      var ctx = canvas.getContext('2d');
      ctx.font = "20px Arial";      // Set font style
      var text = "Ray Yao's Books!";
      var textMetrics = ctx.measureText(text);    // Measure the text
      ctx.fillText(text, 10, 50);    // Draw the text
      ctx.beginPath();    // Draw a line showing the width of the text
      ctx.moveTo(10, 60);
      ctx.lineTo(10 + textMetrics.width, 60);    // Get the text width in pixels
      ctx.strokeStyle = "red";
      ctx.stroke();
   </script>
// Output:
```

---

time type syntax:

<input type="time">

// Used with the <input> element to allow users to select a specific time (hours and minutes).

e.g.

```
<form>
  <label for="appointment-time">Select appointment time:</label>
  <input type="time" id="appointment-time" name="appointment-time">
</form>
```

// Output: Select appointment time: --:--

---

title syntax:

<element title="information">

// Add information about the element

e.g.

```
<p title="book"> PHP Cheat Sheet </p>
```

// Output: PHP Cheat Sheet

---

transform syntax:

transform = "scale() / translate() / rotate()"

// Transform the object in svg.
// scale(width, height) specifies the width and height of the object.
// translate(x, y) moves the object by x-coordinate and y-coordinate.
// rotate(angle) specifies the angle the object will rotate.

e.g.

```
<svg width="200" height="100" >
<text x="20" y="20" fill="blue" transform="scale(1,3)">Hello!</text>
</svg>
```

// Output: Hello!

---

translate() syntax:

context.translate(x, y);

// Moves the canvas' origin to a new location (x, y) from its default position at the top-left corner.

e.g.

```
<canvas id="myCanvas" width="180" height="180" style="border:1px solid black;"></canvas>
  <script>
    var ctx = document.getElementById('myCanvas').getContext('2d');
    ctx.fillStyle = "blue";    // Draw a rectangle without translation
    ctx.fillRect(10, 10, 50, 50);
    ctx.translate(100, 100);    // Translate the canvas by 100 pixels
    ctx.fillStyle = "red";    // Draw a rectangle after translation
    ctx.fillRect(10, 10, 50, 50);
  </script>
```

// Output:

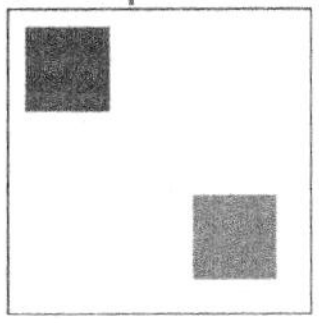

---

type syntax:

<element type="" id="" name="" value="">
// Specify the type of an element, for example:
// type="text / password / button / submit / reset / radio / checkbox / file".
e.g.
Name: <input **type="text"**> <input **type="submit"** value="Submit">
// Output: Name: [   ] [Submit]

---

url type syntax:

<input type="url" name="user-website">
// This is used for input fields where the user is expected to enter a web address (URL).
e.g.
<p>Enter your website URL:</p>
  <form>
    <input **type="url"** id="website" name="website" placeholder="https://example.com">
    <input type="submit" value="Submit">
  </form>
// Output: Enter your website URL:
[https://example.com] [Submit]

---

usemap syntax:

<img src=" " width="" height="" usemap="#mapName"/>
<map name="mapName">
<area shape="" coords="" href="" alt="">
</map>
// "usemap" specifies that the image is applied to <map> by map name.
// <map> defines an image map which contains the <area> elements.
// <area> defines a clickable area inside the <map> element, the <area> can redirect a page to another specified page.
// "shape" specifies the shape of the area.
// "coords" specifies the coordinates of an area in an image map.
// "href" sets the url of the page. "alt" sets an alternate text.
e.g. please see the example of <map> syntax or <area> syntax.

---

value syntax:

<element id="" value="">
// Specify the default value of an element
e.g.
Name: <input type="text" id="name">
* Age: <input type="number" **value="18"**>
Only 18 years old allowed <input type="submit" **value="Submit"**>
// Output:
Name: [   ]
* Age: [18]
Only 18 years old allowed [Submit]

---

volume syntax:

```
video_id.volume=value    // set the video volume ( from 1.0 to 0.0 )
video_id.volume    // check the status of the video volume
```

e.g.

```
<button onclick="fun1()" type="button">Normal Volume</button>
<button onclick="fun2()" type="button">Less Volume</button>
<button onclick="fun3()" type="button">Check Volume</button><br>
<video id="v" width="300" height="180" controls>
  <source src="myVideo.mp4" type="video/mp4">
</video>
<script>
function fun1(){ v.volume =1.0; }    // set normal volume
function fun2(){ v.volume = 0.3; }    // set less volume
function fun3(){ alert( "What is video volume? " + v.volume); }
</script>    // assume that the video volume is set "Less Volume".
```

// Output: [Normal Volume] [Less Volume] [Check Volume]

What is video volume? 0.3

----

week type syntax:

```
<input type="week">
```

// Used with the <input> element to allow users to select a specific week, month and year without choosing a day.

e.g.

```
<form>
  <label for="promotion-week">Select promotion week:</label>
  <input type="week" id="promotion-week" name="promotion-week">
</form>
```

// Output: Select promotion week: [Week --, ----]

----

width syntax:

```
<img src="" width="" height="" alt=""></img>
<iframe src="" width="" height=""></iframe>
<canvas id="" width="" height=""></canvas>
<object data="" width="" height=""></object>
<embed src="" width="" height=""></embed>
<video width="" height="" controls></video>
<input type="image" src="" width="" height="">
```

// Specify the width of the element.

e.g. Please see the examples of above elements.

----

wrap syntax:

```
<textarea wrap="hard/soft">
```

// Specify how to wrap the text in textarea when the form is submitted.

// wrap="hard" or wrap="soft" can set the wrap format of the new page.

Wrap	When the form is submitted:
hard	the wrap format will be submitted too. ("cols" is required)
soft	the wrap format will not be submitted. ("soft" is default)

e.g.

```
<!DOCTYPE html>
<html>
<form action="myFile.php" method="post">    // using PHP
<textarea wrap="hard" name="myWrap" rows="7" cols="28">
"Ray Yao's Books" are useful textbooks for beginners. The straightforward
definitions, the plain examples, the elaborate explanations and the neat layout
feature this helpful and educative book.
</textarea>     // using wrap="hard"
<br><input type="submit">    // PHP will process the submitted data
</form>
</html>
// After submitting, please right click the new page, view page source.
// We can see the result: the new page source keeps the wrap format.
// Output:
```

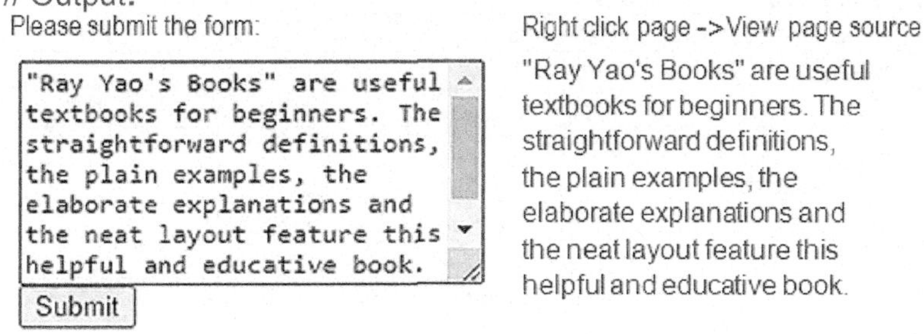

Appendix

Html Tag Chart

Tag	Description
<!--...-->	Defines a comment
<!DOCTYPE>	Defines the document type
<a>	Defines a hyperlink
<abbr>	Defines an abbreviation or an acronym
<acronym>	Defines an acronym
<address>	Defines contact information for the author/owner of a document
<applet>	Defines an embedded applet
<area>	Defines an area inside an image map
<article>	Defines an article
<aside>	Defines content aside from the page content
<audio>	Defines embedded sound content
<b>	Defines bold text
<base>	Specifies the base URL/target for all relative URLs in a document
<basefont>	Specifies a default color, size, and font for all text in a document
<bdi>	Isolates a part of text that might be formatted in a different direction from other text
<bdo>	Overrides the current text direction
<big>	Defines big text
<blockquote>	Defines a section that is quoted from another source
<body>	Defines the document's body
 	Defines a single line break
<button>	Defines a clickable button
<canvas>	Used to draw graphics, on the fly, via scripting (usually JavaScript)
<caption>	Defines a table caption
<center>	Defines centered text
<cite>	Defines the title of a work
<code>	Defines a piece of computer code
<col>	Specifies column properties for each column within a <colgroup> element
<colgroup>	Specifies a group of one or more columns in a table for formatting
<data>	Adds a machine-readable translation of a given content
<datalist>	Specifies a list of pre-defined options for input controls
<dd>	Defines a description/value of a term in a description list
<del>	Defines text that has been deleted from a document
<details>	Defines additional details that the user can view or hide
<dfn>	Specifies a term that is going to be defined within the content
<dialog>	Defines a dialog box or window
<dir>	Defines a directory list
<div>	Defines a section in a document
<dl>	Defines a description list
<dt>	Defines a term/name in a description list
<em>	Defines emphasized text
<embed>	Defines a container for an external application

<fieldset>	Groups related elements in a form
<figcaption>	Defines a caption for a <figure> element
<figure>	Specifies self-contained content
<font>	Defines font, color, and size for text
<footer>	Defines a footer for a document or section
<form>	Defines an HTML form for user input
<frame>	Defines a window (a frame) in a frameset
<frameset>	Defines a set of frames
<h1> to <h6>	Defines HTML headings
<head>	Contains metadata/information for the document
<header>	Defines a header for a document or section
<hgroup>	Defines a header and related content
<hr>	Defines a thematic change in the content
<html>	Defines the root of an HTML document
<i>	Defines a part of text in an alternate voice or mood
<iframe>	Defines an inline frame
<img>	Defines an image
<input>	Defines an input control
<ins>	Defines a text that has been inserted into a document
<kbd>	Defines keyboard input
<label>	Defines a label for an <input> element
<legend>	Defines a caption for a <fieldset> element
<li>	Defines a list item
<link>	Defines the relationship between a document and an external resource
<main>	Specifies the main content of a document
<map>	Defines an image map
<mark>	Defines marked/highlighted text
<menu>	Defines an unordered list
<meta>	Defines metadata about an HTML document
<meter>	Defines a scalar measurement within a known range (a gauge)
<nav>	Defines navigation links
<noframes>	Defines an alternate content for users that do not support frames
<noscript>	Defines an alternate content for users that do not support client-side scripts
<object>	Defines a container for an external application
<ol>	Defines an ordered list
<optgroup>	Defines a group of related options in a drop-down list
<option>	Defines an option in a drop-down list
<output>	Defines the result of a calculation
<p>	Defines a paragraph
<param>	Defines a parameter for an object
<picture>	Defines a container for multiple image resources
<pre>	Defines preformatted text
<progress>	Represents the progress of a task
<q>	Defines a short quotation
<rp>	Defines what to show in browsers that do not support ruby annotations
<rt>	Defines an explanation/pronunciation of characters (for East Asian typography)
<ruby>	Defines a ruby annotation (for East Asian typography)
<s>	Defines text that is no longer correct
<samp>	Defines sample output from a computer program

<script>	Defines a client-side script
<search>	Defines a search section
<section>	Defines a section in a document
<select>	Defines a drop-down list
<small>	Defines smaller text
<source>	Defines multiple media resources for media elements (<video> and <audio>)
<span>	Defines a section in a document
<strike>	Defines strikethrough text
<strong>	Defines important text
<style>	Defines style information for a document
<sub>	Defines subscripted text
<summary>	Defines a visible heading for a <details> element
<sup>	Defines superscripted text
<svg>	Defines a container for SVG graphics
<table>	Defines a table
<tbody>	Groups the body content in a table
<td>	Defines a cell in a table
<template>	Defines a container for content that should be hidden when the page loads
<textarea>	Defines a multiline input control (text area)
<tfoot>	Groups the footer content in a table
<th>	Defines a header cell in a table
<thead>	Groups the header content in a table
<time>	Defines a specific time (or datetime)
<title>	Defines a title for the document
<tr>	Defines a row in a table
<track>	Defines text tracks for media elements (<video> and <audio>)
<tt>	Defines teletype text
<u>	Defines some text that is unarticulated and styled differently from normal text
<ul>	Defines an unordered list
<var>	Defines a variable
<video>	Defines embedded video content
<wbr>	Defines a possible line-break

Html Attribute Chart

Attribute	Description
accept	Specifies the types of files that the server accepts (only for type="file")
accept-charset	Specifies the character encodings that are to be used for the form submission
accesskey	Specifies a shortcut key to activate/focus an element
action	Specifies where to send the form-data when a form is submitted
align	Specifies the alignment according to surrounding elements. Use CSS instead
alt	Specifies an alternate text when the original element fails to display
async	Specifies that the script is executed asynchronously (only for external scripts)
autocomplete	Specifies whether <form> or <input> element should have autocomplete enabled
autofocus	Specifies that the element should automatically get focus when the page loads
autoplay	Specifies that the audio/video will start playing as soon as it is ready
bgcolor	Specifies the background color of an element. Use CSS instead
border	Specifies the width of the border of an element. Use CSS instead
charset	Specifies the character encoding
checked	Specifies that an <input> element should be pre-selected when the page loads
cite	Specifies a URL which explains the quote/deleted/inserted text
class	Specifies one or more class names for an element
color	Specifies the text color of an element. Use CSS instead
cols	Specifies the visible width of a text area
colspan	Specifies the number of columns a table cell should span
content	Gives the value associated with the http-equiv or name attribute
contenteditable	Specifies whether the content of an element is editable or not
controls	Specifies that audio/video controls should be displayed
coords	Specifies the coordinates of the area
data	Specifies the URL of the resource to be used by the object
data-*	Used to store custom data private to the page or application
datetime	Specifies the date and time
default	Specifies that the track is to be enabled if the user do not indicate the another
defer	Specifies that the script is executed when the page has finished parsing
dir	Specifies the text direction for the content in an element
dirname	Specifies that the text direction will be submitted
disabled	Specifies that the specified element/group of elements should be disabled
download	Specifies that the target will be downloaded when a user clicks on the hyperlink
draggable	Specifies whether an element is draggable or not
enctype	Specifies how the form-data should be encoded when submitting it to the server
enterkeyhint	Specifies the text of the enter-key on a virtual keyboard
for	Specifies which form element(s) a label/calculation is bound to
form	Specifies the name of the form the element belongs to
formaction	Specifies where to send the form-data when a form is submitted. for type="submit"
headers	Specifies one or more headers cells a cell is related to
height	Specifies the height of the element
hidden	Specifies that an element is not yet, or is no longer, relevant
high	Specifies the range that is considered to be a high value
href	Specifies the URL of the page the link goes to
hreflang	Specifies the language of the linked document

http-equiv	Provides an HTTP header for the information/value of the content attribute
id	Specifies a unique id for an element
inert	Specifies that the browser should ignore this section
inputmode	Specifies the mode of a virtual keyboard
ismap	Specifies an image as a server-side image map
kind	Specifies the kind of text track
label	Specifies the title of the text track
lang	Specifies the language of the element's content
list	Refers to <datalist> that contains pre-defined options for an <input> element
loop	Specifies that the audio/video will start over again, every time it is finished
low	Specifies the range that is considered to be a low value
max	Specifies the maximum value
maxlength	Specifies the maximum number of characters allowed in an element
media	Specifies what media/device the linked document is optimized for
method	Specifies the HTTP method to use when sending form-data
min	Specifies a minimum value
multiple	Specifies that a user can enter more than one value
muted	Specifies that the audio output of the video should be muted
name	Specifies the name of the element
novalidate	Specifies that the form should not be validated when submitted
onabort	Script to be run on abort
onafterprint	Script to be run after the document is printed
onbeforeprint	Script to be run before the document is printed
onbeforeunload	Script to be run when the document is about to be unloaded
onblur	Script to be run when the element loses focus
oncanplay	Script to be run when a file is ready to start playing
oncanplaythrough	Script run when file can be played all the way to end without pausing for buffering
onchange	Script to be run when the value of the element is changed
onclick	Script to be run when the element is being clicked
oncontextmenu	Script to be run when a context menu is triggered
oncopy	Script to be run when the content of the element is being copied
oncuechange	Script to be run when the cue changes in a <track> element
oncut	Script to be run when the content of the element is being cut
ondblclick	Script to be run when the element is being double-clicked
ondrag	Script to be run when the element is being dragged
ondragend	Script to be run at the end of a drag operation
ondragenter	Script to be run when an element has been dragged to a valid drop target
ondragleave	Script to be run when an element leaves a valid drop target
ondragover	Script to be run when an element is being dragged over a valid drop target
ondragstart	Script to be run at the start of a drag operation
ondrop	Script to be run when dragged element is being dropped
ondurationchange	Script to be run when the length of the media changes
onemptied	Script to be run when something bad happens and the file is suddenly unavailable
onended	Script to be run when the media has reach the end
onerror	Script to be run when an error occurs
onfocus	Script to be run when the element gets focus
onhashchange	Script to be run when there has been changes to the anchor part of the a URL
oninput	Script to be run when the element gets user input
oninvalid	Script to be run when the element is invalid

onkeydown	Script to be run when a user is pressing a key
onkeypress	Script to be run when a user presses a key
onkeyup	Script to be run when a user releases a key
onload	Script to be run when the element is finished loading
onloadeddata	Script to be run when media data is loaded
onloadedmetadata	Script to be run when meta data (like dimensions and duration) are loaded
onloadstart	Script to be run just as the file begins to load before anything is actually loaded
onmousedown	Script to be run when a mouse button is pressed down on an element
onmousemove	Script to be run as long as the mouse pointer is moving over an element
onmouseout	Script to be run when a mouse pointer moves out of an element
onmouseover	Script to be run when a mouse pointer moves over an element
onmouseup	Script to be run when a mouse button is released over an element
onmousewheel	Script to be run when a mouse wheel is being scrolled over an element
onoffline	Script to be run when the browser starts to work offline
ononline	Script to be run when the browser starts to work online
onpagehide	Script to be run when a user navigates away from a page
onpageshow	Script to be run when a user navigates to a page
onpaste	Script to be run when the user pastes some content in an element
onpause	Script to be run when the media is paused either by the user or programmatically
onplay	Script to be run when the media has started playing
onplaying	Script to be run when the media has started playing
onpopstate	Script to be run when the window's history changes.
onprogress	Script to be run when the browser is in the process of getting the media data
onratechange	Script to be run each time the playback rate changes
onredo	Script to be run when a file operation is repeated
onreset	Script to be run when a reset button in a form is clicked.
onresize	Script to be run when the browser window is being resized.
onscroll	Script to be run when an element's scrollbar is being scrolled
onsearch	Script to be run when the user writes something in a search field
onseeked	Script run when seeking attribute is set to false indicating that seeking has ended
onseeking	Script run when the seeking attribute is set to true indicating that seeking is active
onselect	Script to be run when the element gets selected
onstalled	Script run when the browser is unable to fetch the media data for whatever reason
onstorage	Script to be run when a Web Storage area is updated
onsubmit	Script to be run when a form is submitted
onsuspend	Script run when fetching the media data stopped before it is completely loaded
ontimeupdate	Script to be run when the playing position has changed
ontoggle	Script to be run when the user opens or closes the <details> element
onunload	Script to be run when a page has unloaded
onvolumechange	Script to be run each time the volume of a video/audio has been changed
onwaiting	Script to be run when the media has paused but is expected to resume
onwheel	Script to be run when the mouse wheel rolls up or down over an element
open	Specifies that the details should be visible (open) to the user
optimum	Specifies what value is the optimal value for the gauge
pattern	Specifies a regular expression that an <input> element's value is checked against
placeholder	Specifies a short hint that describes the expected value of the element
popover	Specifies a popover element
popovertarget	Specifies which popover element to invoked

popovertargetaction	Specifies what happens to the popover element when the button is clicked
poster	Specifies an image to be shown while the video is downloading, or hits play button
preload	Specifies if and how the author thinks the audio/video should be loaded
readonly	Specifies that the element is read-only
rel	Specifies the relationship between the current document and the linked document
required	Specifies that the element must be filled out before submitting the form
reversed	Specifies that the list order should be descending (9,8,7...)
rows	Specifies the visible number of lines in a text area
rowspan	Specifies the number of rows a table cell should span
sandbox	Enables an extra set of restrictions for the content in an <iframe>
scope	Specifies whether a header cell is a header for a column, row
selected	Specifies that an option should be pre-selected when the page loads
shape	Specifies the shape of the area
size	Specifies the width, in characters or specifies the number of visible options
sizes	Specifies the size of the linked resource
span	Specifies the number of columns to span
spellcheck	Specifies whether the element is to have its spelling and grammar checked or not
src	Specifies the URL of the media file
srcdoc	Specifies the HTML content of the page to show in the <iframe>
srclang	Specifies the language of the track text data (required if kind="subtitles")
srcset	Specifies the URL of the image to use in different situations
start	Specifies the start value of an ordered list
step	Specifies the legal number intervals for an input field
style	Specifies an inline CSS style for an element
tabindex	Specifies the tabbing order of an element
target	Specifies the target for where to open a linked document or where to submit a form
title	Specifies extra information about an element
translate	Specifies whether the content of an element should be translated or not
type	Specifies the type of element
usemap	Specifies an image as a client-side image map
value	Specifies the value of the element
width	Specifies the width of the element
wrap	Specifies how the text in a text area is to be wrapped when submitted in a form

Audio/Video Method Chart

Method / Property	Description
addTextTrack()	Adds a new text track to the audio/video
audioTracks	Returns an AudioTrackList object representing available audio tracks
autoplay	Set or return whether the audio/video should start playing after it is loaded
buffered	Return a TimeRanges object meaning the buffered parts of the audio/video
canPlayType()	Checks if the browser can play the specified audio/video type
controller	Return the MediaController object meaning the current media controller
controls	Sets or returns whether the audio/video should display controls
crossOrigin	Sets or returns the CORS settings of the audio/video
currentSrc	Returns the URL of the current audio/video
currentTime	Sets or returns the current playback position in the audio/video (in seconds)
defaultMuted	Sets or returns whether the audio/video should be muted by default
defaultPlaybackRate	Sets or returns the default speed of the audio/video playback
duration	Returns the length of the current audio/video (in seconds)
ended	Returns whether the playback of the audio/video has ended or not
error	Returns a MediaError object representing the error state of the audio/video
load()	Re-loads the audio/video element
loop	Sets or returns whether the audio/video should start over again when finished
mediaGroup	Sets or returns the group the audio/video belongs to
muted	Sets or returns whether the audio/video is muted or not
networkState	Returns the current network state of the audio/video
pause()	Pauses the currently playing audio/video
paused	Returns whether the audio/video is paused or not
play()	Starts playing the audio/video
playbackRate	Sets or returns the speed of the audio/video playback
played	Return a TimeRanges object representing the played parts of the audio/video
preload	Set or return whether the audio/video should be loaded when the page loads
readyState	Returns the current ready state of the audio/video
seekable	Return a TimeRanges object meaning the seekable parts of the audio/video
seeking	Returns whether the user is currently seeking in the audio/video
src	Sets or returns the current source of the audio/video element
startDate	Returns a Date object representing the current time offset
textTracks	Returns a TextTrackList object representing the available text tracks
videoTracks	Deprecated. Do not use it.
volume	Sets or returns the volume of the audio/video

Audio/Video Event Chart

Event	Description
abort	Fires when the loading of an audio/video is aborted
canplay	Fires when the browser can start playing the audio/video
canplaythrough	Fires when the browser can play through the audio/video without stopping
durationchange	Fires when the duration of the audio/video is changed
emptied	Fires when the current playlist is empty
ended	Fires when the current playlist is ended
error	Fires when an error occurred during the loading of an audio/video
loadeddata	Fires when the browser has loaded the current frame of the audio/video
loadedmetadata	Fires when the browser has loaded meta data for the audio/video
loadstart	Fires when the browser starts looking for the audio/video
pause	Fires when the audio/video has been paused
play	Fires when the audio/video has been started or is no longer paused
playing	Fires when the audio/video is playing after having been paused or stopped
progress	Fires when the browser is downloading the audio/video
ratechange	Fires when the playing speed of the audio/video is changed
seeked	Fires when the user finishes moving/skipping to a new position in audio/video
seeking	Fires when the user starts moving/skipping to a new position in audio/video
stalled	Fires when the browser is trying to get media data, but data is not available
suspend	Fires when the browser is intentionally not getting media data
timeupdate	Fires when the current playback position has changed
volumechange	Fires when the volume has been changed
waiting	Fires when the video stops because it needs to buffer the next frame

Html & Symbol Chart

Symbols	**Please Use Following Codes**
<	<
>	>
&	&
""	" "
©	©
®	®
space	
!	!
;	;

Html Character Sets Chart

Number	ASCII	ANSI	8859-1	UTF-8	Description
32					space
33	!	!	!	!	exclamation mark
34	"	"	"	"	quotation mark
35	#	#	#	#	number sign
36	$	$	$	$	dollar sign
37	%	%	%	%	percent sign
38	&	&	&	&	ampersand
39	'	'	'	'	apostrophe
40	(	(	(	(	left parenthesis
41	)	)	)	)	right parenthesis
42	*	*	*	*	asterisk
43	+	+	+	+	plus sign
44	,	,	,	,	comma
45	-	-	-	-	hyphen-minus
46	.	.	.	.	full stop
47	/	/	/	/	solidus
48	0	0	0	0	digit zero
49	1	1	1	1	digit one
50	2	2	2	2	digit two
51	3	3	3	3	digit three
52	4	4	4	4	digit four
53	5	5	5	5	digit five
54	6	6	6	6	digit six
55	7	7	7	7	digit seven
56	8	8	8	8	digit eight
57	9	9	9	9	digit nine
58	:	:	:	:	colon
59	;	;	;	;	semicolon
60	<	<	<	<	less-than sign
61	=	=	=	=	equals sign
62	>	>	>	>	greater-than sign
63	?	?	?	?	question mark
64	@	@	@	@	commercial at
65	A	A	A	A	A
66	B	B	B	B	B
67	C	C	C	C	C
68	D	D	D	D	D
69	E	E	E	E	E
70	F	F	F	F	F
71	G	G	G	G	G
72	H	H	H	H	H
73	I	I	I	I	I
74	J	J	J	J	J
75	K	K	K	K	K
76	L	L	L	L	L

77	M	M	M	M	M
78	N	N	N	N	N
79	O	O	O	O	O
80	P	P	P	P	P
81	Q	Q	Q	Q	Q
82	R	R	R	R	R
83	S	S	S	S	S
84	T	T	T	T	T
85	U	U	U	U	U
86	V	V	V	V	V
87	W	W	W	W	W
88	X	X	X	X	X
89	Y	Y	Y	Y	Y
90	Z	Z	Z	Z	Z
91	[	[	[	[	left square bracket
92	\	\	\	\	reverse solidus
93	]	]	]	]	right square bracket
94	^	^	^	^	circumflex accent
95	_	_	_	_	low line
96	`	`	`	`	grave accent
97	a	a	a	a	a
98	b	b	b	b	b
99	c	c	c	c	c
100	d	d	d	d	d
101	e	e	e	e	e
102	f	f	f	f	f
103	g	g	g	g	g
104	h	h	h	h	h
105	i	i	i	i	i
106	j	j	j	j	j
107	k	k	k	k	k
108	l	l	l	l	l
109	m	m	m	m	m
110	n	n	n	n	n
111	o	o	o	o	o
112	p	p	p	p	p
113	q	q	q	q	q
114	r	r	r	r	r
115	s	s	s	s	s
116	t	t	t	t	t
117	u	u	u	u	u
118	v	v	v	v	v
119	w	w	w	w	w
120	x	x	x	x	x
121	y	y	y	y	y
122	z	z	z	z	z
123	{	{	{	{	left curly bracket
124	|	|	|	|	vertical line
125	}	}	}	}	right curly bracket

126	~	~	~	~	tilde
127	DEL				
128		€			euro sign
129		□	□	□	NOT USED
130		‚			single low-9 quotation mark
131		ƒ			f with hook
132		„			double low-9 quotation mark
133		…			horizontal ellipsis
134		†			dagger
135		‡			double dagger
136		ˆ			modifier letter circumflex accent
137		‰			per mille sign
138		Š			S with caron
139		‹			single left-pointing angle quotation mark
140		Œ			Latin capital ligature OE
141		□	□	□	NOT USED
142		Ž			Z with caron
143		□	□	□	NOT USED
144		□	□	□	NOT USED
145		‘			left single quotation mark
146		’			right single quotation mark
147		“			left double quotation mark
148		”			right double quotation mark
149		•			bullet
150		–			en dash
151		—			em dash
152		˜			small tilde
153		™			trade mark sign
154		š			s with caron
155		›			single right-pointing angle quotation mark
156		œ			Latin small ligature oe
157		□	□	□	NOT USED
158		ž			z with caron
159		Ÿ			Latin capital letter Y with diaeresis
160					no-break space
161		¡	¡	¡	inverted exclamation mark
162		¢	¢	¢	cent sign
163		£	£	£	pound sign
164		¤	¤	¤	currency sign
165		¥	¥	¥	yen sign
166		¦	¦	¦	broken bar
167		§	§	§	section sign
168		¨	¨	¨	diaeresis
169		©	©	©	copyright sign
170		ª	ª	ª	feminine ordinal indicator
171		«	«	«	left-pointing double angle quotation mark
172		¬	¬	¬	not sign
173		-	-	-	soft hyphen
174		®	®	®	registered sign

175		¯	¯	¯	macron
176		°	°	°	degree sign
177		±	±	±	plus-minus sign
178		^{2}	^{2}	^{2}	superscript two
179		^{3}	^{3}	^{3}	superscript three
180		´	´	´	acute accent
181		µ	µ	µ	micro sign
182		¶	¶	¶	pilcrow sign
183		·	·	·	middle dot
184		¸	¸	¸	cedilla
185		^{1}	^{1}	^{1}	superscript one
186		º	º	º	masculine ordinal indicator
187		»	»	»	right-pointing double angle quotation mark
188		¼	¼	¼	vulgar fraction one quarter
189		½	½	½	vulgar fraction one half
190		¾	¾	¾	vulgar fraction three quarters
191		¿	¿	¿	inverted question mark
192		À	À	À	Latin capital letter A with grave
193		Á	Á	Á	Latin capital letter A with acute
194		Â	Â	Â	Latin capital letter A with circumflex
195		Ã	Ã	Ã	Latin capital letter A with tilde
196		Ä	Ä	Ä	Latin capital letter A with diaeresis
197		Å	Å	Å	Latin capital letter A with ring above
198		Æ	Æ	Æ	Latin capital letter AE
199		Ç	Ç	Ç	Latin capital letter C with cedilla
200		È	È	È	Latin capital letter E with grave
201		É	É	É	Latin capital letter E with acute
202		Ê	Ê	Ê	Latin capital letter E with circumflex
203		Ë	Ë	Ë	Latin capital letter E with diaeresis
204		Ì	Ì	Ì	Latin capital letter I with grave
205		Í	Í	Í	Latin capital letter I with acute
206		Î	Î	Î	Latin capital letter I with circumflex
207		Ï	Ï	Ï	Latin capital letter I with diaeresis
208		Ð	Ð	Ð	Latin capital letter Eth
209		Ñ	Ñ	Ñ	Latin capital letter N with tilde
210		Ò	Ò	Ò	Latin capital letter O with grave
211		Ó	Ó	Ó	Latin capital letter O with acute
212		Ô	Ô	Ô	Latin capital letter O with circumflex
213		Õ	Õ	Õ	Latin capital letter O with tilde
214		Ö	Ö	Ö	Latin capital letter O with diaeresis
215		×	×	×	multiplication sign
216		Ø	Ø	Ø	Latin capital letter O with stroke
217		Ù	Ù	Ù	Latin capital letter U with grave
218		Ú	Ú	Ú	Latin capital letter U with acute
219		Û	Û	Û	Latin capital letter U with circumflex
220		Ü	Ü	Ü	Latin capital letter U with diaeresis
221		Ý	Ý	Ý	Latin capital letter Y with acute
222		Þ	Þ	Þ	Latin capital letter Thorn
223		ß	ß	ß	sharp s

224		à	à	à	a with grave
225		á	á	á	a with acute
226		â	â	â	a with circumflex
227		ã	ã	ã	a with tilde
228		ä	ä	ä	a with diaeresis
229		å	å	å	a with ring above
230		æ	æ	æ	ae
231		ç	ç	ç	c with cedilla
232		è	è	è	e with grave
233		é	é	é	e with acute
234		ê	ê	ê	e with circumflex
235		ë	ë	ë	e with diaeresis
236		ì	ì	ì	i with grave
237		í	í	í	i with acute
238		î	î	î	i with circumflex
239		ï	ï	ï	i with diaeresis
240		ð	ð	ð	eth
241		ñ	ñ	ñ	n with tilde
242		ò	ò	ò	o with grave
243		ó	ó	ó	o with acute
244		ô	ô	ô	o with circumflex
245		õ	õ	õ	o with tilde
246		ö	ö	ö	o with diaeresis
247		÷	÷	÷	division sign
248		ø	ø	ø	o with stroke
249		ù	ù	ù	u with grave
250		ú	ú	ú	u with acute
251		û	û	û	with circumflex
252		ü	ü	ü	u with diaeresis
253		ý	ý	ý	y with acute
254		þ	þ	þ	thorn
255		ÿ	ÿ	ÿ	y with diaeresis

Language Code Chart

Language	ISO Code	Language	ISO Code
Abkhazian	ab	Latin	la
Afar	aa	Latvian (Lettish)	lv
Afrikaans	af	Limburgish (Limburger)	li
Akan	ak	Lingala	ln
Albanian	sq	Lithuanian	lt
Amharic	am	Luga-Katanga	lu
Arabic	ar	Luganda, Ganda	lg
Aragonese	an	Luxembourgish	lb
Armenian	hy	Manx	gv
Assamese	as	Macedonian	mk
Avaric	av	Malagasy	mg
Avestan	ae	Malay	ms
Aymara	ay	Malayalam	ml
Azerbaijani	az	Maltese	mt
Bambara	bm	Maori	mi
Bashkir	ba	Marathi	mr
Basque	eu	Marshallese	mh
Belarusian	be	Moldavian	mo
Bengali (Bangla)	bn	Mongolian	mn
Bihari	bh	Nauru	na
Bislama	bi	Navajo	nv
Bosnian	bs	Ndonga	ng
Breton	br	Northern Ndebele	nd
Bulgarian	bg	Nepali	ne
Burmese	my	Norwegian	no
Catalan	ca	Norwegian bokmål	nb
Chamorro	ch	Norwegian nynorsk	nn
Chechen	ce	Nuosu	ii
Chichewa, Chewa	ny	Occitan	oc
Nyanja	ny	Ojibwe	oj
Chinese	zh	Old Church Slavonic	cu
Chinese (Smpl / Trdtnl)	zh-Hans / zh-Hant	Old Bulgarian	cu
Chuvash	cv	Oriya	or
Cornish	kw	Oromo (Afaan Oromo)	om
Corsican	co	Ossetian	os
Cree	cr	Pāli	pi
Croatian	hr	Pashto, Pushto	ps
Czech	cs	Persian (Farsi)	fa
Danish	da	Polish	pl
Divehi, Dhivehi	dv	Portuguese	pt
Maldivian	dv	Punjabi (Eastern)	pa
Dutch	nl	Quechua	qu
Dzongkha	dz	Romansh	rm
English	en	Romanian	ro
Esperanto	eo	Russian	ru
Estonian	et	Sami	se
Ewe	ee	Samoan	sm
Faroese	fo	Sango	sg
Fijian	fj	Sanskrit	sa
Finnish	fi	Serbian	sr
French	fr	Serbo-Croatian	sh

Fula, Fulah, Pulaar	ff	Sesotho	st
Pular	ff	Setswana	tn
Galician	gl	Shona	sn
Gaelic (Scottish)	gd	Sichuan Yi	ii
Gaelic (Manx)	gv	Sindhi	sd
Georgian	ka	Sinhalese	si
German	de	Siswati	ss
Greek	el	Slovak	sk
Greenlandic	kl	Slovenian	sl
Guarani	gn	Somali	so
Gujarati	gu	Southern Ndebele	nr
Haitian Creole	ht	Spanish	es
Hausa	ha	Sundanese	su
Hebrew	he	Swahili (Kiswahili)	sw
Herero	hz	Swati	ss
Hindi	hi	Swedish	sv
Hiri Motu	ho	Tagalog	tl
Hungarian	hu	Tahitian	ty
Icelandic	is	Tajik	tg
Ido	io	Tamil	ta
Igbo	ig	Tatar	tt
Indonesian	id, in	Telugu	te
Interlingua	ia	Thai	th
Interlingue	ie	Tibetan	bo
Inuktitut	iu	Tigrinya	ti
Inupiak	ik	Tonga	to
Irish	ga	Tsonga	ts
Italian	it	Turkish	tr
Japanese	ja	Turkmen	tk
Javanese	jv	Twi	tw
Kalaallisut, Greenlandic	kl	Uyghur	ug
Kannada	kn	Ukrainian	uk
Kanuri	kr	Urdu	ur
Kashmiri	ks	Uzbek	uz
Kazakh	kk	Venda	ve
Khmer	km	Vietnamese	vi
Kikuyu	ki	Volapük	vo
Kinyarwanda (Rwanda)	rw	Wallon	wa
Kirundi	rn	Welsh	cy
Kyrgyz	ky	Wolof	wo
Komi	kv	Western Frisian	fy
Kongo	kg	Xhosa	xh
Korean	ko	Yiddish	yi, ji
Kurdish	ku	Yoruba	yo
Kwanyama	kj	Zhuang, Chuang	za
Lao	lo	Zulu	zu

Country Code Chart

COUNTRY	ISO Code
AFGHANISTAN	AF
ALBANIA	AL
ALGERIA	DZ
AMERICAN SAMOA	AS
ANDORRA	AD
ANGOLA	AO
ANTARCTICA	AQ
ANTIGUA AND BARBUDA	AG
ARGENTINA	AR
ARMENIA	AM
ARUBA	AW
AUSTRALIA	AU
AUSTRIA	AT
AZERBAIJAN	AZ
BAHAMAS	BS
BAHRAIN	BH
BANGLADESH	BD
BARBADOS	BB
BELARUS	BY
BELGIUM	BE
BELIZE	BZ
BENIN	BJ
BERMUDA	BM
BHUTAN	BT
BOLIVIA	BO
BOSNIA AND HERZEGOVINA	BA
BOTSWANA	BW
BOUVET ISLAND	BV
BRAZIL	BR
BRITISH INDIAN OCEAN TERRITORY	IO
BRUNEI DARUSSALAM	BN
BULGARIA	BG
BURKINA FASO	BF
BURUNDI	BI
CAMBODIA	KH
CAMEROON	CM
CANADA	CA
CAPE VERDE	CV
CAYMAN ISLANDS	KY
CENTRAL AFRICAN REPUBLIC	CF
CHAD	TD
CHILE	CL
CHINA	CN
CHRISTMAS ISLAND	CX
COCOS (KEELING) ISLANDS	CC
COLOMBIA	CO
COMOROS	KM
CONGO	CG
CONGO, THE DEMOCRATIC REPUBLIC OF THE	CD
COOK ISLANDS	CK
COSTA RICA	CR
CÔTE D'IVOIRE	CI

CROATIA	HR
CUBA	CU
CYPRUS	CY
CZECH REPUBLIC	CZ
DENMARK	DK
DJIBOUTI	DJ
DOMINICA	DM
DOMINICAN REPUBLIC	DO
ECUADOR	EC
EGYPT	EG
EL SALVADOR	SV
EQUATORIAL GUINEA	GQ
ERITREA	ER
ESTONIA	EE
ETHIOPIA	ET
FALKLAND ISLANDS (MALVINAS)	FK
FAROE ISLANDS	FO
FIJI	FJ
FINLAND	FI
FRANCE	FR
FRENCH GUIANA	GF
FRENCH POLYNESIA	PF
FRENCH SOUTHERN TERRITORIES	TF
GABON	GA
GAMBIA	GM
GEORGIA	GE
GERMANY	DE
GHANA	GH
GIBRALTAR	GI
GREECE	GR
GREENLAND	GL
GRENADA	GD
GUADELOUPE	GP
GUAM	GU
GUATEMALA	GT
GUINEA	GN
GUINEA-BISSAU	GW
GUYANA	GY
HAITI	HT
HEARD ISLAND AND MCDONALD ISLANDS	HM
HONDURAS	HN
HONG KONG	HK
HUNGARY	HU
ICELAND	IS
INDIA	IN
INDONESIA	ID
IRAN, ISLAMIC REPUBLIC OF	IR
IRAQ	IQ
IRELAND	IE
ISRAEL	IL
ITALY	IT
JAMAICA	JM
JAPAN	JP
JORDAN	JO

KAZAKHSTAN	KZ
KENYA	KE
KIRIBATI	KI
KOREA, DEMOCRATIC PEOPLE'S REPUBLIC OF	KP
KOREA, REPUBLIC OF	KR
KUWAIT	KW
KYRGYZSTAN	KG
LAO PEOPLE'S DEMOCRATIC REPUBLIC (	LA
LATVIA	LV
LEBANON	LB
LESOTHO	LS
LIBERIA	LR
LIBYA, STATE OF	LY
LIECHTENSTEIN	LI
LITHUANIA	LT
LUXEMBOURG	LU
MACAO	MO
MACEDONIA, THE FORMER YUGOSLAV REPUBLIC OF	MK
MADAGASCAR	MG
MALAWI	MW
MALAYSIA	MY
MALDIVES	MV
MALI	ML
MALTA	MT
MARSHALL ISLANDS	MH
MARTINIQUE	MQ
MAURITANIA	MR
MAURITIUS	MU
MAYOTTE	YT
MEXICO	MX
MICRONESIA, FEDERATED STATES OF	FM
MOLDOVA, REPUBLIC OF	MD
MONACO	MC
MONGOLIA	MN
MONTENEGRO	ME
MONTSERRAT	MS
MOROCCO	MA
MOZAMBIQUE	MZ
MYANMAR	MM
NAMIBIA	NA
NAURU	NR
NEPAL, FEDERAL DEMOCRATIC REPUBLIC OF	NP
NETHERLANDS	NL
NETHERLANDS ANTILLES	AN
NEW CALEDONIA	NC
NEW ZEALAND	NZ
NICARAGUA	NI
NIGER	NE
NIGERIA	NG
NIUE	NU
NORFOLK ISLAND	NF
NORTHERN MARIANA ISLANDS	MP
NORWAY	NO
OMAN	OM

PAKISTAN	PK
PALAU	PW
PALESTINE, STATE OF	PS
PANAMA	PA
PAPUA NEW GUINEA	PG
PARAGUAY	PY
PERU	PE
PHILIPPINES	PH
PITCAIRN	PN
POLAND	PL
PORTUGAL	PT
PUERTO RICO	PR
QATAR	QA
RÉUNION	RE
ROMANIA	RO
RUSSIAN FEDERATION	RU
RWANDA	RW
SAINT HELENA	SH
SAINT KITTS AND NEVIS	KN
SAINT LUCIA	LC
SAINT PIERRE AND MIQUELON	PM
SAINT VINCENT AND THE GRENADINES	VC
SAMOA	WS
SAN MARINO	SM
SAO TOME AND PRINCIPE	ST
SAUDI ARABIA	SA
SENEGAL	SN
SERBIA	RS
SEYCHELLES	SC
SIERRA LEONE	SL
SINGAPORE	SG
SLOVAKIA	SK
SLOVENIA	SI
SOLOMON ISLANDS	SB
SOMALIA	SO
SOUTH AFRICA	ZA
SOUTH GEORGIA AND THE SOUTH SANDWICH ISLANDS	GS
SOUTH SUDAN	SS
SPAIN	ES
SRI LANKA	LK
SUDAN	SD
SURINAME	SR
SVALBARD AND JAN MAYEN	SJ
SWAZILAND	SZ
SWEDEN	SE
SWITZERLAND	CH
SYRIAN ARAB REPUBLIC	SY
TAIWAN	TW
TAJIKISTAN	TJ
TANZANIA, UNITED REPUBLIC OF	TZ
THAILAND	TH
TIMOR-LESTE	TL
TOGO	TG
TOKELAU	TK

TONGA	TO
TRINIDAD AND TOBAGO	TT
TUNISIA	TN
TURKEY	TR
TURKMENISTAN	TM
TURKS AND CAICOS ISLANDS	TC
TUVALU	TV
UGANDA	UG
UKRAINE	UA
UNITED ARAB EMIRATES	AE
UNITED KINGDOM	GB
UNITED STATES	US
UNITED STATES MINOR OUTLYING ISLANDS	UM
URUGUAY	UY
UZBEKISTAN	UZ
VANUATU	VU
VENEZUELA	VE
VIET NAM	VN
VIRGIN ISLANDS, BRITISH	VG
VIRGIN ISLANDS, U.S.	VI
WALLIS AND FUTUNA	WF
WESTERN SAHARA	EH
YEMEN	YE
ZAMBIA	ZM
ZIMBABWE	ZW

Html Sandbox Chart

Sandbox Allow	**Sandbox Restrict**
empty or no value set	prevent form submission
allow-forms	disabled all script running
allow-modals	disable apis
allow-orientation-lock	display content as if it's from unique origin
allow-pointer-lock	disabled links from targeting tab or window
allow-popups	prevent content to navigate to iframe's page
allow-popups-to-escape-sandbox	disable automatic triggered events (autoplay)
allow-presentation	prevent form submission
allow-same-origin	
allow-scripts	
allow-top-navigation	
allow-top-navigation-by-user-activation	

Http Messages Chart

Message:	Description:
100 Continue	The server has received the request headers, and the client should proceed to send the request body
101 Switching Protocols	The requester has asked the server to switch protocols
103 Early Hints	Used with the Link header to allow the browser to start preloading resources while the server prepares a response
200 OK	The request is OK (this is the standard response for successful HTTP requests)
201 Created	The request has been fulfilled, and a new resource is created
202 Accepted	The request has been accepted for processing, but the processing has not been completed
203 Non-Authoritative Information	The request has been successfully processed, but is returning information that may be from another source
204 No Content	The request has been successfully processed, but is not returning any content
205 Reset Content	The request has been successfully processed, but is not returning any content, and requires that the requester reset the document view
206 Partial Content	The server is delivering only part of the resource due to a range header sent by the client
300 Multiple Choices	A link list. The user can select a link and go to that location. Maximum five addresses
301 Moved Permanently	The requested page has moved to a new URL
302 Found	The requested page has moved temporarily to a new URL
303 See Other	The requested page can be found under a different URL
304 Not Modified	Indicates the requested page has not been modified since last requested
307 Temporary Redirect	The requested page has moved temporarily to a new URL
308 Permanent Redirect	The requested page has moved permanently to a new URL
400 Bad Request	The request cannot be fulfilled due to bad syntax
401 Unauthorized	The request was a legal request, but the server is refusing to respond to it. For use when authentication is possible but has failed or not yet been provided
402 Payment Required	*Reserved for future use*
403 Forbidden	The request was a legal request, but the server is refusing to respond to it
404 Not Found	The requested page could not be found but may be available again in the future

405 Method Not Allowed	A request was made of a page using a request method not supported by that page
406 Not Acceptable	The server can only generate a response that is not accepted by the client
407 Proxy Authentication Required	The client must first authenticate itself with the proxy
408 Request Timeout	The server timed out waiting for the request
409 Conflict	The request could not be completed because of a conflict in the request
410 Gone	The requested page is no longer available
411 Length Required	The "Content-Length" is not defined. The server will not accept the request without it
412 Precondition Failed	The precondition given in the request evaluated to false by the server
413 Request Too Large	The server will not accept the request, because the request entity is too large
414 Request-URI Too Long	Server will not accept the request, because the URI is too long. Occurs when you convert a POST request to a GET request with a long query information.
415 Unsupported Media Type	The server will not accept the request, because the media type is not supported
416 Range Not Satisfiable	The client has asked for a portion of the file, but the server cannot supply that portion
417 Expectation Failed	The server cannot meet the requirements of the Expect request-header field
500 Internal Server Error	A generic error message, given when no more specific message is suitable
501 Not Implemented	The server either does not recognize the request method, or it lacks the ability to fulfill the request
502 Bad Gateway	The server was acting as a gateway or proxy and received an invalid response from the upstream server
503 Service Unavailable	The server is currently unavailable (overloaded or down)
504 Gateway Timeout	The server was acting as a gateway or proxy and did not receive a timely response from the upstream server
505 HTTP Version Not Supported	The server does not support the HTTP protocol version used in the request
511 Network Authentication Required	The client needs to authenticate to gain network access

Ascii Code Chart

Character	Code	Description
space	32	space
!	33	exclamation mark
"	34	quotation mark
#	35	number sign
$	36	dollar sign
%	37	percent sign
&	38	ampersand
'	39	apostrophe
(	40	left parenthesis
)	41	right parenthesis
*	42	asterisk
+	43	plus sign
,	44	comma
-	45	hyphen
.	46	period
/	47	slash
0	48	0
1	49	1
2	50	2
3	51	3
4	52	4
5	53	5
6	54	6
7	55	7
8	56	8
9	57	9
:	58	colon
;	59	semicolon
<	60	less-than
=	61	equals-to
>	62	greater-than
?	63	question mark
@	64	at sign
A	65	A
B	66	B
C	67	C
D	68	D
E	69	E
F	70	F
G	71	G
H	72	H
I	73	I
J	74	J
K	75	K
L	76	L
M	77	M
N	78	N
O	79	O
P	80	P
Q	81	Q

<table>
<tr><td>R</td><td>82</td><td>R</td></tr>
<tr><td>S</td><td>83</td><td>S</td></tr>
<tr><td>T</td><td>84</td><td>T</td></tr>
<tr><td>U</td><td>85</td><td>U</td></tr>
<tr><td>V</td><td>86</td><td>V</td></tr>
<tr><td>W</td><td>87</td><td>W</td></tr>
<tr><td>X</td><td>88</td><td>X</td></tr>
<tr><td>Y</td><td>89</td><td>Y</td></tr>
<tr><td>Z</td><td>90</td><td>Z</td></tr>
<tr><td>[</td><td>91</td><td>left square bracket</td></tr>
<tr><td>\</td><td>92</td><td>backslash</td></tr>
<tr><td>]</td><td>93</td><td>right square bracket</td></tr>
<tr><td>^</td><td>94</td><td>caret</td></tr>
<tr><td>_</td><td>95</td><td>underscore</td></tr>
<tr><td>`</td><td>96</td><td>grave accent</td></tr>
<tr><td>a</td><td>97</td><td>a</td></tr>
<tr><td>b</td><td>98</td><td>b</td></tr>
<tr><td>c</td><td>99</td><td>c</td></tr>
<tr><td>d</td><td>100</td><td>d</td></tr>
<tr><td>e</td><td>101</td><td>e</td></tr>
<tr><td>f</td><td>102</td><td>f</td></tr>
<tr><td>g</td><td>103</td><td>g</td></tr>
<tr><td>h</td><td>104</td><td>h</td></tr>
<tr><td>i</td><td>105</td><td>i</td></tr>
<tr><td>j</td><td>106</td><td>j</td></tr>
<tr><td>k</td><td>107</td><td>k</td></tr>
<tr><td>l</td><td>108</td><td>l</td></tr>
<tr><td>m</td><td>109</td><td>m</td></tr>
<tr><td>n</td><td>110</td><td>n</td></tr>
<tr><td>o</td><td>111</td><td>o</td></tr>
<tr><td>p</td><td>112</td><td>p</td></tr>
<tr><td>q</td><td>113</td><td>q</td></tr>
<tr><td>r</td><td>114</td><td>r</td></tr>
<tr><td>s</td><td>115</td><td>s</td></tr>
<tr><td>t</td><td>116</td><td>t</td></tr>
<tr><td>u</td><td>117</td><td>u</td></tr>
<tr><td>v</td><td>118</td><td>v</td></tr>
<tr><td>w</td><td>119</td><td>w</td></tr>
<tr><td>x</td><td>120</td><td>x</td></tr>
<tr><td>y</td><td>121</td><td>y</td></tr>
<tr><td>z</td><td>122</td><td>z</td></tr>
<tr><td>{</td><td>123</td><td>left curly brace</td></tr>
<tr><td>|</td><td>124</td><td>vertical bar</td></tr>
<tr><td>}</td><td>125</td><td>right curly brace</td></tr>
<tr><td>~</td><td>126</td><td>tilde</td></tr>
</table>

Html Character Chart

Character	Code	Entity Name	Description
space			non-breaking space
¡	¡	¡	inverted exclamation mark
¢	¢	¢	cent
£	£	£	pound
¤	¤	¤	currency
¥	¥	¥	yen
¦	¦	¦	broken vertical bar
§	§	§	section
¨	¨	¨	spacing diaeresis
©	©	©	copyright
ª	ª	ª	feminine ordinal indicator
«	«	«	angle quotation mark left
¬	¬	¬	negation
-			soft hyphen
®	®	®	registered trademark
¯	¯	¯	spacing macron
°	°	°	degree
±	±	±	plus-or-minus
^{2}	²	²	superscript 2
^{3}	³	³	superscript 3
´	´	´	spacing acute
µ	µ	µ	micro
¶	¶	¶	paragraph
•	·	·	middle dot
¸	¸	¸	spacing cedilla
^{1}	¹	¹	superscript 1
º	º	º	masculine ordinal indicator
»	»	»	angle quotation mark right
¼	¼	¼	fraction 1/4
½	½	½	fraction 1/2
¾	¾	¾	fraction 3/4
¿	¿	¿	inverted question mark

Html Rel Value Chart

VALUE	DESCRIPTION
nofollow	Specifies the link is not endorsed or is not controlled by the current page's author. Note: search engines often ignore links with nofollow.
noopener	No information about the current page is sent to the linked page. Used for untrusted links to avoid tampering with the current page.
noreferrer	Prevents the browser from sending referrer data about the current page.
stylesheet	Specifies that the link is a stylesheet to be added to the page.
icon	Specifies that the link is an icon (favicon or otherwise) that represents the page.
canonical	Specifies the preferred URL for the current page.
dns-prefetch	Specifies to perform pre-emptive DNS resolution for the linked resource.
external	Indicates the link is to a page outside the current site (different domain).
author	Specifies the link it to a page about the current page's author.
help	Specifies the link is to a context-sensitive help page.
license	Specifies the link is to a page with licensing information.
prev	Specifies the previous page in a series of pages.
next	Specifies the next page in a series of pages.
bookmark	Indicates the link is apermalink that can be used for bookmarking.
search	Specifies the link is to a search page for the current page.
alternate	Specifies the link is to an alternative version of the page. For example, a different device type, or other language version.
tag	Specifies a tag keyword for the current page, i.e. a word that identifies the current page.

Canvas Functions

Canvas Functions	Descriptions
beginPath()	Begins a path or resets the current path.
clearRect(x, y, width, height)	Clears the specified rectangle.
clip()	Clips a region of any shape and size from the canvas.
closePath()	Closes the current path.
createImageData(width, height)	Creates a new, blank ImageData object.
createLinearGradient(x0, y0, x1, y1)	Creates a linear gradient.
createPattern(image, repetition)	Creates a pattern using the specified image.
createRadialGradient(x0, y0, r0, x1, y1, r1)	Creates a radial gradient.
drawImage(image, x, y)	Draws an image on the canvas at specified coordinates.
drawImage(image, x, y, width, height)	Draws an image with the specified width and height.
fill()	Fills the current path.
fillRect(x, y, width, height)	Draws a filled rectangle.
fillStyle = color	Sets the color for the fill.
fillText(text, x, y)	Draws filled text at the specified position.
getImageData(x, y, width, height)	Returns an ImageData object that copies the pixel data.
globalAlpha = value	Sets the transparency level.
globalCompositeOperation = type	Sets the drawing order of shapes and images.
isPointInPath(x, y)	Checks if the specified point is inside the current path.
lineTo(x, y)	Draws a straight line to the specified point.
lineWidth = width	Sets the width of lines.
measureText(text)	Returns the width of the specified text.
moveTo(x, y)	Moves the path to the specified point without drawing.
putImageData(imageData, x, y)	Puts the image data (ImageData) back onto the canvas.
rect(x, y, width, height)	Draws a rectangle.
rotate(angle)	Rotates the canvas.
scale(x, y)	Scales the canvas horizontally and vertically.
setTransform(a, b, c, d, e, f)	Resets the matrix, then applies the transformation.
stroke()	Draws the outline of the current path.
strokeRect(x, y, width, height)	Draws a rectangle outline.
strokeStyle = color	Sets the color for the stroke (outline).
strokeText(text, x, y)	Draws text with an outline.
transform(a, b, c, d, e, f)	Multiply the current matrix by the matrix from arguments
translate(x, y)	Moves the canvas and its origin to a different point.

Css Color Chart

Color Name	HEX	Color Name	HEX
AliceBlue	#F0F8FF	LightSalmon	#FFA07A
AntiqueWhite	#FAEBD7	LightSeaGreen	#20B2AA
Aqua	#00FFFF	LightSkyBlue	#87CEFA
Aquamarine	#7FFFD4	LightSlateGray	#778899
Azure	#F0FFFF	LightSteelBlue	#B0C4DE
Beige	#F5F5DC	LightYellow	#FFFFE0
Bisque	#FFE4C4	Lime	#00FF00
Black	#000000	LimeGreen	#32CD32
BlanchedAlmond	#FFEBCD	Linen	#FAF0E6
Blue	#0000FF	Magenta	#FF00FF
BlueViolet	#8A2BE2	Maroon	#800000
Brown	#A52A2A	MediumAquaMarine	#66CDAA
BurlyWood	#DEB887	MediumBlue	#0000CD
CadetBlue	#5F9EA0	MediumOrchid	#BA55D3
Chartreuse	#7FFF00	MediumPurple	#9370DB
Chocolate	#D2691E	MediumSeaGreen	#3CB371
Coral	#FF7F50	MediumSlateBlue	#7B68EE
CornflowerBlue	#6495ED	MediumSpringGreen	#00FA9A
Cornsilk	#FFF8DC	MediumTurquoise	#48D1CC
Crimson	#DC143C	MediumVioletRed	#C71585
Cyan	#00FFFF	MidnightBlue	#191970
DarkBlue	#00008B	MintCream	#F5FFFA
DarkCyan	#008B8B	MistyRose	#FFE4E1
DarkGoldenRod	#B8860B	Moccasin	#FFE4B5
DarkGray	#A9A9A9	NavajoWhite	#FFDEAD
DarkGreen	#006400	Navy	#000080
DarkKhaki	#BDB76B	OldLace	#FDF5E6
DarkMagenta	#8B008B	Olive	#808000
DarkOliveGreen	#556B2F	OliveDrab	#6B8E23
DarkOrange	#FF8C00	Orange	#FFA500
DarkOrchid	#9932CC	OrangeRed	#FF4500
DarkRed	#8B0000	Orchid	#DA70D6
DarkSalmon	#E9967A	PaleGoldenRod	#EEE8AA
DarkSeaGreen	#8FBC8F	PaleGreen	#98FB98
DarkSlateBlue	#483D8B	PaleTurquoise	#AFEEEE
DarkSlateGray	#2F4F4F	PaleVioletRed	#DB7093
DarkTurquoise	#00CED1	PapayaWhip	#FFEFD5

DarkViolet	#9400D3	PeachPuff	#FFDAB9
DeepPink	#FF1493	Peru	#CD853F
DeepSkyBlue	#00BFFF	Pink	#FFC0CB
DimGray	#696969	Plum	#DDA0DD
DodgerBlue	#1E90FF	PowderBlue	#B0E0E6
FireBrick	#B22222	Purple	#800080
FloralWhite	#FFFAF0	Red	#FF0000
ForestGreen	#228B22	RosyBrown	#BC8F8F
Fuchsia	#FF00FF	RoyalBlue	#4169E1
Gainsboro	#DCDCDC	SaddleBrown	#8B4513
GhostWhite	#F8F8FF	Salmon	#FA8072
Gold	#FFD700	SandyBrown	#F4A460
GoldenRod	#DAA520	SeaGreen	#2E8B57
Gray	#808080	SeaShell	#FFF5EE
Green	#008000	Sienna	#A0522D
GreenYellow	#ADFF2F	Silver	#C0C0C0
HoneyDew	#F0FFF0	SkyBlue	#87CEEB
HotPink	#FF69B4	SlateBlue	#6A5ACD
IndianRed	#CD5C5C	SlateGray	#708090
Indigo	#4B0082	Snow	#FFFAFA
Ivory	#FFFFF0	SpringGreen	#00FF7F
Khaki	#F0E68C	SteelBlue	#4682B4
Lavender	#E6E6FA	Tan	#D2B48C
LavenderBlush	#FFF0F5	Teal	#008080
LawnGreen	#7CFC00	Thistle	#D8BFD8
LemonChiffon	#FFFACD	Tomato	#FF6347
LightBlue	#ADD8E6	Turquoise	#40E0D0
LightCoral	#F08080	Violet	#EE82EE
LightCyan	#E0FFFF	Wheat	#F5DEB3
LightGoldenRodYellow	#FAFAD2	White	#FFFFFF
LightGray	#D3D3D3	WhiteSmoke	#F5F5F5
LightGreen	#90EE90	Yellow	#FFFF00
LightPink	#FFB6C1	YellowGreen	#9ACD32

Css Selector Chart

Selectors	Examples
#id	#user (select the element with id="user")
.class	.fruit (select all elements with class="fruit")
element.class	p.fruit (select only <p> elements with class="fruit")
*	* {color:red} (select all elements)
element	div {color: red} (select all <div> elements)
group	h1, h2, h3 {color: red} (select h1, h2, h3)
descendant	div li {color: red} (select li that is a descendant of div)
descendant	p* (select all elements within a p element)
child	div>p {color: red} (select p that is a direct child of div)
adjacent sibling	h1 + p {color: red} (select p that follows h1)
general sibling	h2 ~ p {color: red} (select all p that shares h2)
attribute	a[href] {color: red} (select all a that includes href)
attribute value	a[href="ok"] {color: red} (select all a that includes href & ok)
class attribute	p.fruit (select p element with a class attribute "fruit")
id attribute	p#fruit (select p element with an id attribute "fruit")
class attribute val	p[class] (select p element with a class attribute of any value)
class attribute val	p[class="v"] (select p element with a class attribute value "v")
:active	a:active (Select the active link)
:visited	a:visited (Select all visited links)
:link	a:link (Select all unvisited links)
:hover	a:hover (Select links on mouse over
:root	:root (Select the document's root element)
:not(selector)	:not(p) (Select any non <p> elements)
:valid	input:valid (Select all input elements with a valid value)
:checked	input:checked (Select all checked <input> element)
:required	input:required (Select <input> with "required" attribute)

Css Property Chart

Property	Description
align-content	specify alignment of contents within flex container.
align-items	specify default alignment of items within flex container.
align-self	specify alignment of selected items within flex container.
animation	specify key-frame-based animations.
animation-delay	specify when animation will start.
animation-direction	specify if animation played in reverse on alternate cycles
animation-duration	specify seconds an animation taken to complete cycle.
animation-fill-mode	specify how a css animation applying styles to its target
animation-iteration-count	specify number of times of animation cycle before stop
animation-name	specify name of animations applied to selected element.
animation-play-state	specify whether animation is running or paused.
animation-timing-function	specify how an animation runs duration of each cycle.
backface-visibility	specify back side of a transformed element visible
background	define a background property within one declaration
background-attachment	specify background image fixed in viewport or scrolls.
background-clip	specify painting area of background.
background-color	define an element's background color.
background-image	define an element's background image.
background-origin	specify positioning area of background images.
background-position	define origin of a background image.
background-repeat	specify whether/how background image is tiled.
background-size	specify size of background images.
border	set width, style, and color for an element's border.
border-bottom	set width, style, and color of bottom border of element.
border-bottom-color	set color of bottom border of an element.
border-bottom-left-radius	define shape of bottom-left border corner of an element.
border-bottom-right-radius	define shape of bottom-right border corner of an element.
border-bottom-style	set style of bottom border of an element.
border-bottom-width	set width of bottom border of an element.
border-collapse	specify if a cell borders are connected or separated.
border-color	set color of border on all four sides of an element.
border-image	specify how an image used in place of border styles.

border-image-outset	specify how border image extends beyond border box.
border-image-repeat	specify if image-border repeated, rounded or stretched.
border-image-slice	specify inward offsets of image-border.
border-image-source	specify location of image to be used as a border.
border-image-width	specify width of image-border.
border-left	set width, style, and color of left border of an element.
border-left-color	set color of left border of an element.
border-left-style	set style of left border of an element.
border-left-width	set width of left border of an element.
border-radius	define shape of border corners of an element.
border-right	set width, style, and color of right border of an element.
border-right-color	set color of right border of an element.
border-right-style	set style of right border of an element.
border-right-width	set width of right border of an element.
border-spacing	set spacing between borders of adjacent table cells.
border-style	set style of border on all four sides of an element.
border-top	set width, style, and color of top border of an element.
border-top-color	set color of top border of an element.
border-top-left-radius	define shape of top-left border corner of an element.
border-top-right-radius	define shape of top-right border corner of an element.
border-top-style	set style of top border of an element.
border-top-width	set width of top border of an element.
border-width	set width of border on all four sides of an element.
bottom	specify location of bottom edge of positioned element.
box-shadow	applies one or more drop-shadows to element's box.
box-sizing	alter default css box model.
caption-side	specify position of table's caption.
clear	specify the flow next to floated elements
clip	define clipping region.
color	specify color of text of an element.
column-count	specify number of columns in a multi-column element.
column-fill	specify how columns will be filled.
column-gap	specify gap between columns in a multi-column element.
column-rule	specify a straight line, or "rule", to be drawn in columns
column-rule-color	specify color of rules drawn between columns
column-rule-style	specify style of rule drawn between columns

column-rule-width	specify width of rule drawn between columns
column-span	specify how many columns an element spans across
column-width	specify optimal width of columns in a multi-column item.
columns	set column-width and column-count properties.
content	inserts generated content.
counter-increment	increments one or more counter values.
counter-reset	creates or resets one or more counters.
cursor	specify type of cursor.
direction	define text direction/writing direction.
display	specify how an element is displayed onscreen.
empty-cells	show or hide borders, backgrounds of empty cells.
flex	specify components of a flexible length.
flex-basis	specify initial main size of flex item.
flex-direction	specify direction of flexible items.
flex-flow	set flex-direction and flex-wrap properties.
flex-grow	specify how flex item will grow relative to other items
flex-shrink	specify how flex item will shrink relative to other items
flex-wrap	specify whether flexible items should wrap or not.
float	specify whether or not a box should float.
font	define a variety of font properties within one declaration.
font-family	define a list of fonts for element.
font-size	define font size for text.
font-size-adjust	preserves readability of text when font fallback occurs.
font-stretch	selects a normal, condensed, expanded face of a font.
font-style	define font style for text.
font-variant	specify font variant.
font-weight	specify font weight of text.
height	specify height of an element.
justify-content	specify how flex item is aligned with axis of flex container
left	specify location of left edge of positioned element.
letter-spacing	set extra spacing between letters.
line-height	set height between lines of text.
list-style	define display style for a list and list elements.
list-style-image	specify image to be used as a list-item marker.
list-style-position	specify position of list-item marker.
list-style-type	specify marker style for a list-item.

margin	set margin on all four sides of element.
margin-bottom	set bottom margin of element.
margin-left	set left margin of element.
margin-right	set right margin of element.
margin-top	set top margin of element.
max-height	specify maximum height of an element.
max-width	specify maximum width of an element.
min-height	specify minimum height of an element.
min-width	specify minimum width of an element.
opacity	specify transparency of an element.
order	specify order in which a flex item is shown and laid out
outline	set width, style, color for all sides of an item's outline.
outline-color	set color of outline.
outline-offset	set space between an outline and border edge of item
outline-style	set a style for an outline.
outline-width	set width of outline.
overflow	specify treatment of content that overflows item's box.
overflow-x	specify treatment of content that overflows horizontally.
overflow-y	specify treatment of content that overflows vertically.
padding	set padding on all four sides of element.
padding-bottom	set padding to bottom side of an element.
padding-left	set padding to left side of an element.
padding-right	set padding to right side of an element.
padding-top	set padding to top side of an element.
page-break-after	insert a page breaks after an element.
page-break-before	insert a page breaks before an element.
page-break-inside	insert a page breaks inside an element.
perspective	define perspective by which child elements are viewed.
perspective-origin	define origin for perspective property.
position	specify how an element is positioned.
quotes	specify quotation marks for embedded quotations.
resize	specify whether or not an element is resizable by user.
right	specify location of right edge of positioned element.
tab-size	specify length of tab character.
table-layout	specify a table layout algorithm.
text-align	set horizontal alignment of inline content.

text-align-last	specify how last line of a block is aligned
text-decoration	specify decoration added to text.
text-decoration-color	specify color of text-decoration-line.
text-decoration-line	specify what line decorations are added to element.
text-decoration-style	specify style of text-decoration-line property
text-indent	indent first line of text.
text-justify	specify justification method to use when setting align
text-overflow	specify how text content shown, when overflows
text-shadow	applies one or more shadows to text content
text-transform	transforms case of text.
top	specify location of top edge of positioned element.
transform	applies a 2d or 3d transformation to an element.
transform-origin	define origin of transformation for an element.
transform-style	specify how nested elements are rendered in 3d space.
transition	define transition between two states of an element.
transition-delay	specify when transition effect will start.
transition-duration	specify number of seconds of a transition effect
transition-property	specify names of css properties of a transition effect
transition-timing-function	specify speed curve of transition effect.
vertical-align	set vertical positioning of an element
visibility	specify whether or not an element is visible.
white-space	specify how white space inside element is handled.
width	specify width of an element.
word-break	specify how to break lines within words.
word-spacing	set spacing between words.
word-wrap	specify whether to break words when content overflows
z-index	specify a layering or stacking order of positioned item

Css Structure Chart

Inline Style CSS <tag style = “attribute: value”>......</tag>
Internal Style CSS <style type = “text/css”> </style>
Set Style for Tag <style type = “text/css”> tag {attribute: value} </style>
Set Style for ID <style type = “text/css”> #id {attribute: value} </style>
Set Style for Class <style type = “text/css”> .class {attribute: value} </style>
Set Style for Tag’s ID <style type = “text/css”> tag #id {attribute: value} </style>
Set Style for Tag’s Class <style type = “text/css”> tag .class {attribute: value} </style>
Link External Style <link rel = “stylesheet” type = “text/css” title = “External File” href = “myStyle.css” >
Import External Style @import “myStyle1.css”; @import “myStyle2.css”; @import “myStyle3.css”;

Css Functions Chart

Function	Description
attr()	Returns the value of an attribute of the selected element
calc()	Allows you to perform calculations to determine CSS property values
conic-gradient()	Creates a conic gradient
counter()	Returns the current value of the named counter
cubic-bezier()	Defines a Cubic Bezier curve
hsl()	Defines colors using the Hue-Saturation-Lightness model (HSL)
hsla()	Defines colors using the Hue-Saturation-Lightness-Alpha model (HSLA)
linear-gradient()	Creates a linear gradient
max()	Uses the highest value from a comma-separated list as the property value.
min()	Uses the smallest value from a comma-separated list as the property value.
radial-gradient()	Creates a radial gradient
repeating-conic-gradient()	Repeats a conic gradient
repeating-linear-gradient()	Repeats a linear gradient
repeating-radial-gradient()	Repeats a radial gradient
rgb()	Defines colors using the Red-Green-Blue model (RGB)
rgba()	Defines colors using the Red-Green-Blue-Alpha model (RGBA)
var()	Inserts the value of a custom property

Recommended Books by Ray Yao

(**Note:** Each Cheat Sheet contains more than 300 examples, more than 300 outputs, and more than 300 explanations.)

Printed in Great Britain
by Amazon

59403062R00097